INVESTING FOR NEWBIES

INVESTING FOR NEWBIES

What You Need to Know to Get Started

ROLAN H. CARREON M.D.

2014

DISCLAIMER

To my doctor colleagues --

In spite of what we earn or what others assume we earn, we are still self-employed individuals; that means "no work, no pay" for us. We don't have paid vacation and sick leaves. We don't have security of tenure. We don't have unemployment benefits. We don't have retirement benefits. Our income is never guaranteed. Over the long term, our income does not consistently grow. In fact, it has to fall off at some point, as new doctors come in.

We need financial planning more than ever.

Contents

Preface

Often, people become interested in investing when they hear about a certain "must-buy" stock or a great performing fund. Others will be convinced to put money in certain investments recommended by friends or family. Others will hear about someone who struck it big in the markets and will try to replicate what that person has done. Of course, not every investor will be successful. Many will realize that they do not even have the funds to invest. Many will also have to withdraw their money prematurely because they have some expenses to take care of. Many will be surprised at the amount of taxes, commissions and fees that they eventually have to pay. Many will realize that some investments will require considerable time, effort, and skill which they are incapable of providing. Many will eventually lose money and regret their decisions Many unsuccessful investors will blame their advisers, even if they fully consented to the investment strategy. Some will be too traumatized to ever invest again, even if they actually still need to.

Everybody needs financial planning. As a self-employed professional, who doesn't have legally mandated, financial safety nets that a conventionally employed person enjoys, I probably need financial planning more. This situation is what persuaded me to learn about investments.

My journey in studying investments is an interesting one. I initially kept my new passion a secret, but when a photograph of myself, endorsing an investment course, came out in newspapers, my new hobby was exposed.

My co-doctors then started to ask me about investments, but I never really gave them proper answers, because there are just so many things that need to be said. This is what prompted me to write this book.

This book initially started as a free flow of ideas, comments, and personal stories, which I then had to edit and organize to something more informational and practical. Despite the use of many investment terminologies, I did my best to come up with a final product that is concise and understandable for newbie investors.

Since I work as a doctor, I currently don't work in finance. I wrote this book from a perspective of an outsider looking in, which turned out to be a good thing since most newbie investors are in the same situation anyway.

I hope this book gives you the information you need to start investing. As they say... information is money.

RHCarreon

Rolan H. Carreon, MD MBA
Philippines, 2014

1

INVESTMENT CONCEPTS

mmm eggs...
But why are they all in one basket?

By investing, what do you plan to achieve?

Ask anyone about his reason for investing, and the most likely answer will be "To make as much money as I can". That doesn't really fly in the investment world. Great gains can be achieved by winning the lottery, but the probability of that happening is very small. An investor has to give reasons that are more specific and realistic. For an investment strategy to be formulated, an investor must give a realistic range of how much he wants to make (known as **returns**) and when he plans to make them (known as the **investment horizon**). What the investor wants to achieve, or his **return objective**, must be realistic given the limits of the investment strategy and the ensuing investment portfolio. Those limits, **risk tolerance** and **constraints**, make the return objective investor-specific. It is not correct to imitate someone's return objective when your circumstances differ.

"Know what you own,
and know why you own it."

- Peter Lynch

How much risk can you and are willing to take?

Some investors have specific circumstances which enable them to take risks. This refers to the investor's **ability** to take risks. Some investors have behavioral traits which make them more inclined to take risks. This refers to the investor's **willingness** to take risks.

One's investment strategy should be based on both his ability and willingness to take risks. For example, people who spend only a small fraction of their income have the ability to take risks. Even if they lose money on their investments, their lifestyles and spending habits won't be significantly affected. Young and able-bodied persons also have the ability to take risks. Even if they lose money on their investments, they still have a lot of time to potentially earn back that money. Although some investors have the ability to take risks, they may not be willing to. It is not uncommon to see rich young individuals (who have the ability to take risks) keep most of their money in bank accounts for fear of losing them in more risky investments. Both the ability and willingness comprise the investor's **risk tolerance.**

The Risk/Return Trade-off

This trade-off is the reason why an investor has to determine his return objective and risk tolerance. The investor needs to balance these two out.

If one wants to earn high returns, then he must be willing to accept higher risks. If one wants to keep risks low, then he must be willing to accept potentially lower returns. An investment with a high return but with low risk does not exist. If such a thing existed, it probably did so only temporarily since investors would have consumed it right away, thereby removing it from the market.

...the best way to spot investment fraud is the promise of safety and high returns. If someone offers you this, turn 180 degrees and do not walk – run.
--- William Bernstein, "The Four Pillars of Investing"(2002)

Rational vs. Irrational Investment Behavior

Many investment and economic theories presume that investors act in a rational manner. Unfortunately, investors, being human, do not always act that way. An investor must discover his own biases (these biases, whether cognitive or emotional, lead to irrational investment behaviors) and adapt to or minimize them. The previous example of a rich, young individual who keeps most of his money in a savings account is exhibiting irrational investment behavior. A good financial adviser will always seek out these biases (and determine the reasons behind them), so that he can educate and advise his clients better. If your financial adviser is not interested in profiling your behavior, look for someone else who is.

An investor should also be aware of the irrational behaviors exhibited by other investors. An investor can use this knowledge to his advantage.

> *"The fact that people will be full of greed, fear or folly is predictable. The sequence is not predictable."*
> *- Warren Buffett*

Borrowing, Saving, Investing

Borrowing is using at present time, the money you'll earn in the future. Suppose you plan to buy a house worth five million. You don't have that much in your bank account. With an income of 500,000 yearly, you expect to earn that amount in ten years. Since you want and need your own house right now, you'll borrow the amount and pay it in installments as you earn the money in the future.

Saving is using in the future, the money that you have earned. You want to buy a house worth five million ten years from now. You may have that amount in your bank account now or you expect to earn the full amount within ten years. Either way, the key here is earning the money prior to utilization.

Investing may involve both borrowing and saving. Investing and borrowing are not mutually exclusive. In fact, borrowing is a strategy to raise investment funds. The use of borrowed money for investment purposes is known as **leverage**. Corporations use leverage to grow their businesses. A real estate investor, who takes out a bank loan to purchase property, is using leverage. In currency and derivatives trading, leverage is also prevalent. Lending, the complement of borrowing, is actually a major investment strategy (e.g. fixed income investments or bonds). Only interest bearing loans qualify as investments. The interest-free PHP 1,000 you lent your friend was not an investment. Of course, friendships are investments in themselves, though in this book, I will not cover those types.

Investing is somewhat similar to saving. Like saving, investment involves utilization of the full value of whatever you have at the end of the earning period. I wrote full value since a portion of the investment can be utilized within the investment period. Stock dividends (for equity), interests (for bonds), rent (for real estate) are examples of partial values received within the investment period that can be utilized by the investor. However, the full values of those investments can only be utilized once the stocks are sold/traded/exchanged, the bonds mature or are sold/traded/exchanged, and the real properties are sold/traded/exchanged.

Unlike saving though, investing requires the expectation of **appreciation**. Putting money in your piggy bank is saving, not investing. Putting your money in an actual bank where it will earn interest is investing (yes, even if it is traditionally called a savings account). Take note that I used the word expectation with regards to appreciation. When you invest, you expect and hope to make money. Unfortunately, you may make money, lose money or break even.

Value appreciation of your investment refers to the important investment concept of **RETURN**. Return refers to how much your investment appreciated in value over a given period of time. Return will also include the portion of the investment that you received during the investment period such as dividends, interests, rent, etc.

The difference between the expected and actual return refers to the important investment concept of **RISK**. For example, you plan to buy a share of stock that is expected to have a yearly return of 6%. On the first year, the stock yielded 6%. On the second year, the stock yielded only 2%. On the third year, the stock lost 5%. Those differences describe the risk of the stock. The more variable the returns of the investment, the riskier it is.

The Concept of Interest

If someone were to give you PHP 1,000, would you rather receive it now or one year later? Money is more valuable now than in the future. This is because money can be invested at present so that it may have a higher value in the future. The above demonstrates the time value of money.

When you allow others to use your money at present with the promise to return it to you in the future, you expect the borrower to compensate you for using your money. When you put your money in a savings account, you plan to use your money in the future. In the meantime, the bank can use your money to lend to its clients. The bank compensates you for that privilege. On the flipside, if you are the borrower, you have to compensate the lender for using his money.

The compensation for using another entity's money for a certain period is called **INTEREST.**

Interest is often expressed as a rate rather than the actual money value. Interest rate is the percentage of the principal that the borrower pays the lender for a given period. For a loan of PHP 1000 with 10% annual interest, the borrower will have to pay PHP 100 yearly. For a loan of PHP 1000 with 2% quarterly interest, the borrower will have to pay PHP 20 every three months. In finance, unless otherwise specified, interest rates are expressed as annual rates.

The interest rate directly varies with risk. This is in accordance with the risk-return trade-off principle. A lender willing to take higher risks should expect higher returns.

The most important risk that a lender faces is that the borrower may default on his debt. The borrower may either be unable or unwilling to pay his debt. This refers to **credit risk**. The likelihood that a borrower will settle his debt is known as his credit worthiness.

The longer the loan period, the higher the risk. This is because the lender will not have access to his money for a longer period of time. This refers to **liquidity risk**.

The less credit worthy the borrower, the higher the risk; hence, the higher interest rate. The longer the term of the loan, the higher the risk; hence, the higher interest rate. I will discuss both credit and liquidity risks in latter sections.

Banks are authorized and highly regulated agents of the Central Bank; therefore, they are very credit worthy with regards to their role to hold our deposits. The government also guarantees deposits to a certain extent. These are reasons why our deposits carry minimal interests. In fact, demand deposits (also known as checking accounts) often do not carry interest. Savings accounts, which the bank expects to hold longer than checking accounts, carry some interest. Time deposits, which have holding terms, carry higher interest than ordinary savings accounts. The longer the period of the time deposit, the higher the rate. The higher interest is due to the reduced liquidity.

If you borrow money from banks, the interest rate you'll pay will be the bank's lending rate. Most conventional loans from local banks are guaranteed loans (backed by collateral) so they carry relatively low interest rates. Credit card loans, which are non-guaranteed bank loans, carry significantly higher interest rates.

Interest rates for deposits and loans are often set by individual banks based on the **prevailing interest rates**. The prevailing interest rate is set by the monetary authority of a particular country. In the Philippines, the monetary authority is the Central Bank. The Central Bank sets the prevailing interest rates depending on its monetary policy and strategy; which in turn are influenced by long and short term, actual and expected, economic conditions.

The deposit and lending rates of banks are called **commercial rates** . These are based on the the prevailing rates, with adjustments for terms of transactions, credit worthiness of borrowers, and the banks' business and competitive strategies.

The change in prevailing rates and the ensuing changes in commercial rates are significant sources of risk for many investors.

The Power of Compounded Interest

Interest earned can either be taken out or reinvested. Interest reinvested will eventually earn interest on itself. Earning subsequent interest on reinvested interest is known as **compounding**.

Let's take for example an initial investment of 100 which earns 10% interest yearly. After one year, the investment will earn 10. If the 10 is reinvested, the total investment will then be 110 and the interest after another year will be 11. If the 11 is again reinvested, the total investment will be 121 and the interest earned after another year will be 12.1. Therefore, after three years, the initial 100 investment becomes 133.1.

If the investor withdraws the interests yearly, the investment amount will remain at 100 and the yearly interest will only be 10. Without compounding, total interests earned on the investment after three years will only be 30. With compounding, interests earned will have a total of 33.1. As demonstrated above, as the duration of investment increases, the added value of compounding versus non-compounding also increases.

Without compounding, that is when interest is taken out, interest earned grows linearly through time. With compounding, that is when interest is reinvested, interest earned grows exponentially.

The previous example showed annual compounding. In actual practice, interests are paid more frequently. Interest on deposits are paid quarterly while interest on bonds are usually paid semi-annually. If compounding is done more frequently, the value added due to compounding increases.

An initial investment of 100 with 10% annual interest, compounded yearly for three years will yield 33.1%

An initial investment of 100 with 10% annual interest, compounded semiannually for three years will yield 34.01%. The yield semiannually will be 5% (half of the 10%) compounded over six periods (3 years x 2 periods/year).

An initial investment of 100 with 10% annual interest, compounded quarterly for three years will yield 34.49%. The yield quarterly will be 2.5% (quarter of 10%) compounded over twelve periods (3 years x 4 periods/year).

Consequently, when the compounding is done semi-annually or quarterly, the actual interest rate paid annually is greater than the quoted 10% annual rate because of intra-year compounding. For the example above:

Semi-annual payment = Actual annual
interest rate of 10.25 %
Quarterly payment = Actual annual interest
rate of 10.38%.

The actual interest rate earned due to intra-year compounding is the **effective annual rate** or EAR. The EAR will be higher the more frequent the compounding.

A good example of the above is the interest earned on savings accounts. A savings account, which pays interest quarterly, with a quoted annual interest of 1%, will actually earn 1.0038% in a year if no withdrawals are made. Take note that the effective annual interest is gross of taxes. In the Philippines, 20% of interest earned is withheld as tax. The tax is taken out from the account and therefore not reinvested. The after tax interest earned is 0.8024%, versus just 0.8000% without compounding.

Deposit accounts are examples of investments where interest compounds. Some investments, like coupon bonds, do not have compounded interests since the interests are regularly paid out and never reinvested. Because coupon bonds do not allow for reinvestment, they have **reinvestment risk**. With zero coupon bonds, the interests are compounded.

Stocks do not have compounded interests since there are no interest payments from them to begin with. The closest analogy for stocks would be the concept of **retained earnings.** This is when companies use some, or all of the profits to grow the company, instead of paying them all as dividends to stockholders.

Rule of 72

The rule of 72 is a commonly used estimation technique in determining how many years an investment will double if compounded annually at a corresponding interest rate. The number 72 is derived from the following formula:

$$2 = (1 + r)^T$$

- where T is the number of periods given the corresponding interest rate r. If the rate given is the annual interest rate, then T corresponds to years.

The number of years the investment will double is 72 divided by the annual interest rate. A PHP 100 initial investment earning 8% annually is expected to become PHP 200 in 72/8 or 9 years. Rule of 72 is only used for estimation purposes since the actual doubling time will be different mathematically (though close). 100 growing at 8% annual compounded interest will be 199.90 in 9 years; so the actual doubling time is just a tad longer. Consequently, as the compounding periods become more frequent, the doubling time also shortens.

Double your money accounts used to be popular in the Philippines when interest rates were a lot higher. Banks used to offer five-year double your money deposit accounts. Using the rule of 72, the annual rate was around 14.4%. That's very high in today's investment climate, so those are no longer offered.

Liquidity

Liquidity, in layman's terms, refers to the quick convertibility of a financial instrument to cash, without or with very minimal change in value. Cash, of course, is the most liquid financial instrument. Its face value is its trading value.

An example of an illiquid asset is real estate. It may take a seller months or years to find a buyer willing to pay the asking price. If a seller wants to liquidate the property quickly, he has to bear any or a combination of the following costs:

- Decrease his asking price to make the property more sellable; in this case the property may be bought quickly, but the value paid to the seller will be less than the original asking value

- Get a broker; the property may be sold at the asking price, but the value paid to the seller will be decreased by the broker's commission

- Agree to installment payments for the property; in this case, even if the property is sold at the asking price, the full value will only be realized by the seller in the future

Investments such as time deposits and mutual funds also have liquidity charges. If an investor wants to liquidate those assets immediately, early withdrawal penalties will be deducted from the investments.

The higher the value of an investment, the more illiquid it becomes. For example, an item worth 100,000 is more difficult to sell than an item worth 100. This is the reason why real estate is illiquid.

Stocks have varying degrees of liquidity. A blue chip stock traded in the stock exchange is considered very liquid. A low cap growth stock, though traded in the stock exchange, is not as liquid. A privately held stock (not traded in the stock exchange) is usually illiquid.

The liquidity of any investment is inversely related to the difference between the asking price of the seller and the bid price of the buyer.

If the difference between the ask and bid prices is minimal or none, the investment is liquid. If the difference is large, then that investment has low liquidity. An investment with no offers from buyers is illiquid.

Foreign currencies also have varying degrees of liquidity. The US dollar (USD), the most traded currency with the Philippine Peso (PHP) is liquid. The bid and ask prices do not differ by much. For currencies that are less traded; such as the Euro and British Pound; the difference between the buy and sell prices (percentage wise) are wider than that of USD:PHP, reflecting their lower liquidities. Currencies that are not directly traded with PHP (such as South American currencies) have much lower liquidities.

The Benefit of Asset Diversification

"Don't put your eggs in one basket" is the financial advice you'll often hear. It is best to put your money (eggs) into different investment assets (baskets) so that if one asset drops in value, losses will be limited.

There is a compelling explanation for risk diversification, and that explanation is a mathematical one!

How Portfolio Return is Computed

Returns vary from time to time for a given asset. To get the asset return over a given period, the **MEAN** return is computed. The portfolio return is therefore the weighted average of the mean returns of each portfolio asset.

Example: Portfolio AB consists of two investments, A and B. There is an equal amount of money in both. A has a mean return of 10%. B has an mean return of 20%. What is the return of portfolio AB?

Weight of Investment A = 0.50
Weight of Investment B = 0.50
Return of A = 0.10
Return of B = 0.20

Return of Portfolio AB =
(0.5 X 0.1) + (0.5 X 0.2) = 0.15 or 15%

How Portfolio Risk is Computed

Returns will vary from the mean return from time to time. Remember that risk refers to the variability of returns; therefore, to get the asset risk over that period, the **STANDARD DEVIATION** is computed.

Example: Portfolio AB consists of two investments, A and B. There is an equal amount of money in both. A has a risk of 10%. B has a risk of 20%. What is the risk of portfolio AB?

How do we compute for portfolio standard deviation?

From what we learned from **Statistics**, the standard deviation of AB combined is the **square root** of the formula below:

(wA x wA x sdA x sdA) + (wB x wB x sdB x sdB) + (2 x wA x wB x sdA x sdB x p A,B)

where:

wA = weight of A
wB = weight of B
sdA = standard deviation of A
sdB = standard deviation of B
p A, B = correlation coefficient between A and B

The **correlation** between returns of assets A and B is an important variable in determining the the overall risk for portfolio AB.

If assets A and B are perfectly positively correlated (p A, B = 1); by plugging the variables in the given formula, the standard deviation of portfolio AB will equal to 0.15 or 15%. 15% is also the weighted average of the risks of A and B.

If assets A and B are not at all correlated (p A, B = 0); the standard deviation of portfolio AB will only be 0.112 or 11.2%.

If assets A and B are perfectly negatively correlated (p A, B = -1); the standard deviation of portfolio AB will only be 0.05 or 5%.

Based on the above, the portfolio risk becomes less (compared to the weighted average risk) as the correlation between the assets decreases. The calculations for the combined risk of three or more assets become more complicated, but the general pattern remains the same.

In reality, different assets are not perfectly correlated, and may even have low correlation. If someone invests in a variety of assets, he can reduce overall portfolio risk.

However, the risk reduction benefit with diversification declines as the number of assets increases. Risk reduction by going from a two asset portfolio to a three asset one is greater than the risk reduction by going from a thirty nine asset portfolio to a forty asset one. Some experts peg the sweet spot at around thirty assets.

2

INVESTMENT ASSET
CLASSES

Traditional and Alternative Asset Classes

Investments can be grouped into traditional and alternative classes. Stocks, bonds, and cash investments are considered traditional. Other types of investments are considered alternative.

Mutual funds are pooled funds that are usually invested in traditional assets.

Compared to traditional asset classes, alternative investments are usually less liquid. These investments are also more challenging to value.

Alternative investments usually have higher returns on their own, so they enhance the returns of the overall portfolio. They also have low correlation with traditional asset classes, so they provide portfolio risk reduction via diversification.

2.1

STOCKS

Bull Market

Bear Market

Prices of securities are rising or are expected to rise.
There is widespread investor optimism.

Prices of securities are falling for long periods.
There is widespread investor pessimism.

"One of the funny things about the stock market is that every time one person buys, another sells, and both think they are astute. "
- William Feather

What are Stocks?

People would often associate investments with stocks. Stocks (also known as shares, equity) are financial securities that represent ownership of a particular company.

Why do companies need to be subdivided into shares? First, because most companies are owned by multiple individuals, the company's ownership structure must reflect that. Second, whole companies are difficult to trade in toto. It will be too expensive to buy and sell whole companies. It will also be time consuming since all owners must agree to the trade.

Stocks can be traded privately or publicly. Publicly traded stocks are traded in what is commonly known as the **stock market.**

Types of Stocks

Common shares – These are stocks that represent true ownership of a company. The investor takes the advantages (e.g. voting rights) and disadvantages (e.g. risks) that come with ownership. As the company increases in value (as long as the number of shares remain constant), the value of the common stocks also increases. A common stock investor usually has a right to vote. Common shareholders may also receive dividends, though dividends may not be issued all the time.

However, if the company loses value (as long as the number of shares remain constant) the value of the common stocks also falls. When the company goes bankrupt or closes, shareholders of common stocks have last dibs on the company's assets.

Preferred shares – These are hybrids of ownership and debt. Preferred shareholders often cannot vote. The hallmark of preferred shares is that they pay out fixed predetermined dividends, and these must be paid as agreed upon, regardless of company performance. This is what makes preferred shares debt-like. This is also the reason why the share values remain constant. The dividends are similar to interest payments that must be paid when due, and they must be paid first before common share dividends. This is what makes them "preferred".

The difference with debt is that preferred shares do not have terms; hence, these shares do not mature. In debt, the issuer is obligated to pay the principal at maturity. With preferred shares, the issuer is not obligated to buy back the shares.

Convertible preferred shares – These are preferred stocks that can be exchanged for a predetermined amount of common shares after a predetermined date.

Stocks not traded publicly fall under **private equity**. Private equity is an alternative asset class.

The stock market benefits both the companies and the investing public.

Benefits For The Listed Companies:

The companies will have access to funds from the public. A company, needing outside funds to grow, may seek out loans or private investors. However, loans (and bonds) require payment of fixed obligations (interests and subsequent principal payment). Private investors may require significant ownership, which may result in less control for the current owners. A company listing itself in the stock market will have access to public investor funds without the precondition of fixed obligations (as in loans) or significant ownership (as in private equity).

Benefits For The Investing Public:

The investing public will have the chance to own a piece of these listed corporations. Normally, an investor needs a large amount to buy into these companies privately. When these companies go public, even small-time investors can buy into them.

Since the stock market imposes strict rules on financial reporting, the investing public will have access to information they need to trade these companies' stocks.

The stock market provides liquidity; since it brings together buyers and sellers, and facilitates easy and low cost trading.

The liquidity of the stock market enables **price discovery**. Since the stocks are traded frequently by anonymous parties, the trading prices will approximate the stocks' fair values.

Trading in the stock market has **tax advantages**. Investors are often exempted from the high capital gains and documentary stamp taxes that are charged for private stock transactions. In the Philippines, public stocks that meet the minimum float requirement enjoy these tax reliefs when traded.

Initial Public Offering

The process when the company first issues stocks in exchange for public funds is known as the IPO or Initial Public Offering.

Public investors can commit to buying stocks for IPO during the **subscription period**. When the number of shares the public investors commit to is greater than the number of shares offered, the IPO is said to be **oversubscribed**.

Issuing companies don't actually sell the IPO shares directly to public investors since these issuing companies do not have the capabilities, expertise, and resources in dealing with investors. These companies will normally require the services of **underwriters**.

The underwriter is a financial institution (typically a large bank or investment firm) which will buy all the IPO shares from the company and then sell them to the public. These underwriters (which are themselves large institutional investors) may keep some shares for their own portfolios. These underwriters procure the shares at lower than IPO rates; the differences are their fees.

If you are interested in subscribing to an IPO, you go to the brokerage firm or bank (it is not uncommon for one IPO to have many underwriters) that underwrites the offering.

The IPO share price is based on the projected value of the company's equity (including the effect of the fresh IPO funds on the company's growth) as computed by financial analysts involved in that particular IPO. When the shares start trading in the stock market, the stock price will then be determined solely by market demand.

Stocks are priced based on a company's **expected long term** performance.

A company that grew its profits by 5% for this year will NOT necessarily see an increase in the price of its stock. If the company is expected to grow its profits by 10%, the stock price will most likely fall. If the company is expected to grow its profits by only 2%, the stock price will most likely rise.

A company whose profits plunged by 5% for this year will NOT necessarily see a decrease in the price of its stock. If the company is expected to have a decline in its profits by 10%, the stock price will most likely rise. If the company is expected to have a profit decline by only 2%, the stock price will most likely fall.

The stock price of a company will most likely rise when it performs better than expected or "less bad" than expected. The stock price of a company will most likely fall when it performs worse than expected or "less good" than expected.

Notice that I used the term "most likely" in the preceding paragraphs. This is because changes in stock prices may not even be related to the company's business performance at all. There are many investors who buy and sell stocks based on the stock's price trend over time, without ever checking up on the company's actual business performance. Some investors may prematurely sell stocks that are expected to perform well because of the need for liquidity. Some trade based on their love or hate for the companies. For example, many investors avoid stocks of tobacco companies.

The unpredictability, variability and irrationality in investor behavior are somewhat responsible for the fluctuations in stock prices. If investor behaviors are perfectly rational, stock prices will easily converge to their intrinsic values.

How Stocks Trade

Stocks have two prices. The price, that the current holders are willing to sell the stock for, is the **ASK** price. The price, that the potential buyers are willing to buy it for, is the **BID** price.

The ask price is usually higher than the bid price, and as long as this is the case, the stock will not be traded.

If demand for a stock increases, more investors will be willing to buy the stock at a higher price. If the investor's bid price rises enough to match the higher ask price, the stock is traded. This new price will be higher than the price for which the stock previously traded.

If many owners suddenly want to offload a particular stock, more owners will be willing to sell the stock at lower prices. If the owner's ask price declines enough to match the lower bid price, the stock is traded. This new price will be lower than the price for which the stock previously traded.

The ask and buy prices of a stock may differ amongst several traders. For example, an investor wanting to buy 1000 shares for PHP 50 each, may be able to buy only 500 shares at that price. To fill the order, the investor may need to pay higher prices (e.g. PHP 51 for the next 300 shares and PHP 52 for the last 200 shares) to other sellers.

Computers now do the work of matching orders from sellers and buyers. Traders shouting at each other in the exchange floor is a thing of the past.

At the end of trading day, four prices will be reported for each stock:

The opening price or OPEN – the price for which the stock first trades on that day
The closing price or CLOSE – the price for which the stock last trades on that day
The highest intra-day price or HIGH (or HI) – the highest price for which the stock trades on that day
The lowest intra-day price or LOW (or LO) – the lowest price for which the stock trades on that day

The **CLOSE** is the most often reported price to mainstream investors. This is usually compared to the previous trading day's close to determine whether the stock is a **gainer** or a **loser**. Many analysts also chart the closing prices of a stock over time to summarize a stock's performance for that period.

The **OPEN** is the price that usually determines how the stock will perform during the day. This price will often reflect market sentiment for a particular stock after trading hours. A stock which interest investors after trading hours (probably due to information that is made available at that time), will usually have a higher open price.

The intra-day **HIGH** and **LOW** prices can mean a number of things. Large swings and reversals in high and low prices reflect volatility. If the high price is equal to the closing price, this means that there is a sustained demand for the stock. If the high price is higher than both the closing and opening prices; this means that there was high demand initially for the stock during trading, but this demand waned and reversed (some investors may have believed that the stock became overpriced during trading, or may have sold their stocks to cash in on the profit they already made that day), leading to a lower close.

If the low price is equal to the close, this means that there is a sustained sell-off of the stock during the day. If the low is lower than both opening and closing prices, this means that there was an initial sell-off of the stock, but investors (sensing a bargain) began to buy the stock again.

VOLUME is a very important component of stock trade reporting. The true volume of the stock trade is not the number of shares traded but the monetary value. 1000 shares of stock A, trading at 10 cents each, have a monetary value of only 100; while 10 shares of stock B, trading at 2,500 each, have a monetary value of 25,000. A larger volume of stock B traded, despite less shares actually changing hands.

Volume is a determinant of a stock's liquidity. The more the stock is traded, the more liquid it becomes.

Stock Market Index

Stock market indices are measures that describe particular segments of the stock market or the stock market as a whole.

The media often report these indices to reflect the performance of the general economy or a specific sector of the economy. Because actual economic indicators; such as GDP, inflation, unemployment rates, etc are not reported daily; the media often use these indices to describe general economic performance. However, the stock market does not actually reflect current economic performance, since stock prices rise and fall based on long term expectations.

The most well known local stock index is the PSEi (formerly known as the PHISIX). This index represents the adjusted (from a historical base number when the PHISIX was first introduced), weighted (with weights according to the market capitalization of the component stocks) average of the component stocks. The PSEi's components are 30 largely capitalized, highly liquid (commonly termed blue-chip) companies.

There is a less known local index, the PSE All-Shares Index. This index represents most stocks in the PSE. Like the PSEi, the All-Shares is the weighted average of the market capitalization of the component stocks, adjusted from a historical base number.

These indices are often used by investors as **benchmarks,** meaning investors compare the performance of their own stock investments to the performance of the stock market indices that reflect their investment strategy.

Benchmarking

An investor needs to know how his investments did based on certain benchmarks. A stock market index with component stocks similar to the components of an investor's stock portfolio qualifies as a benchmark. Benchmarks are available measures that reflect the investor's investment strategy.

If you are an investor that has a very well diversified Philippine stock portfolio (large, mid and small cap companies from all sectors), then the All-Shares may be an appropriate benchmark.

Let's say that for this year, your portfolio gained 10%, is that good? Not necessarily. If the All-Shares (your benchmark) gained by 20%, then your portfolio underperformed. If your portfolio lost 5%, is that bad? Not necessarily. If the benchmark lost 10%, then your portfolio overperformed the benchmark.

Creating your own portfolio requires considerable resources; money (fees for research and financial advisers who will create your portfolio), effort and time (if you are creating the portfolio yourself).

If you are busy with another job and you have to divert your time and effort to create and adjust your portfolio, then these activities represent additional opportunity costs.

Despite all the resources spent on creating your own portfolio, and you still end up with a portfolio that underperforms your benchmark, wouldn't it have been more convenient and less costly if you just mimic the benchmark? The decision here is not clearcut, since the benchmark may be costly and difficult to replicate. Buying up and rebalancing periodically all the components of the All-Shares index will require significant transaction costs.

The benchmark should reflect your investment strategy. If you are an investor focused on the energy and communications sectors only, then the PSEi and All-Shares are not appropriate benchmarks. The problem is that the appropriate benchmarks may not always be available.

Benchmarks are proxies for the overall market performances of the corresponding investment strategies. For investors trading large cap stocks, a large cap stock index represents the collective performance of investors with that strategy. Investors who overperform the benchmark also overperform most investors with the similar strategy. For underperformance, the same logic applies.

How to Make Money in the Stock Market

The answer is very simple. **Buy undervalued** stocks and **sell overvalued** stocks.

Unfortunately, it is challenging, specially for newbie investors, to determine which stocks are undervalued or overvalued.

Ways to Determine if a Stock is Undervalued or Overvalued:

Compare the Stock's Market Value with Its Intrinsic Value

Investors may consult financial analysts' reports. The brokerage firm (you are trading with) may provide you with free reports. Financial analysts estimate the intrinsic values of the stocks they follow. If the intrinsic value is higher than the market value, the stock is undervalued. If the intrinsic value is lower than the market value, the stock is overvalued. If the intrinsic and market values are equal, the stock is fairly valued.

Financial analysts often differ in their estimations. A stock may be overvalued to one analyst and undervalued to another. If faced with this dilemma, some investors search for the consensus opinion.

Unfortunately, an ordinary person will not have the expertise nor the resources to determine whether a stock is over, under or fairly valued. To be able to value a company, one must have access to external data (economic, market, and industry reports, etc.) and internal data (financial statements, dividend policies, growth strategies, etc.) and must be able to analyze them to come up with an estimate. All that effort goes to the analysis of just one stock. Imagine doing that for more for than a hundred different stocks. The above type of analysis is known as **fundamental analysis**.

Compare the Relative Values of Stocks Belonging to the Same Industry

The **Price to Earnings ratio** or PE ratio is the most often quoted ratio for this purpose. The Price here refers to the market price, while the Earnings represent the net profit of the company.

The PE ratio, like some ratios used for stock analysis, is a measure of a company's **relative value**. For example, company A which has earnings of PHP 1 per share and a stock price of PHP 15, has a PE ratio of 15. If other companies in the same industry have PE ratios higher than 15, company A is undervalued. If other companies in the same industry have PE ratios lower than 15, company A is overvalued.

It is important to compare only companies within the same industry since each industry will have their own range of PE ratios.

Companies in the technology industry often have high PE ratios, while those in the utility industry often have low ratios. Therefore, choosing between a tech stock and utility stock based on their PE ratios won't make sense.

Observe and Analyze the Stock's Trading Pattern Over Time

The process of observing and studying the trading patterns of a stock in order to predict future trading activity is known as **technical analysis**.

Technical analysts observe the price and volume trading patterns of stocks and try to predict the future prices based on these patterns. For example, a technical analyst might deem that a stock that has been trading at successively lower prices over the past few days is already undervalued and may be due for a price increase anytime soon.

On the flipside, an analyst might deem that a stock that has been trading very high in recent weeks is already overvalued and may be due for a price decline.

Technical analysis is relatively easier and faster to perform than fundamental analysis. This is why some newbie investors feel confident in performing technical analysis even without the help of financial experts.

Hold, Buy or Sell Recommendations

If a stock is just slightly over or undervalued, many analysts do not recommend trading because the costs involved may negate the gains derived from the trade. In the above situations, and in cases of fairly valued stocks, the analyst gives **HOLD** recommendations.

For stocks that are significantly undervalued, around 10% or more for most analysts, the analyst gives **BUY** recommendations. For stocks that are significantly overvalued, the analyst gives **SELL** recommendations.

The analyst might use any, a combination, or all three methods of analysis; fundamental, relative value, and technical; as bases for his recommendations.

Timing Stock Investments

It is difficult enough for an investor to determine WHICH stocks are undervalued or overvalued. The investor also needs to determine WHEN they are maximally so, so he can act before anybody else does. Therefore, stock trading is not just about stock-picking, it is also about timing.

Money can be lost with poor timing. For example, a stock is trading at PHP 10 and is estimated to be undervalued (intrinsic value at 15). Seasoned investors may jump on the stock right away and buy it at 10.

As buying continues, the price may rise to 13. An investor who buys the stock at this time will eventually earn only 2, while the early investors will earn 5. The late investor might be happy that he gained 2; but in reality, he lost a potential income of 3.

Sometimes, an undervalued stock may continue to fall in price before recovering. Using the same stock example, the early investors might buy the stock at 10 before it falls further down to 8. A late investor buying the stock at 8 will earn 7 as the stock reaches its intrinsic value of 15. The early investors will gain 5 but lose potential income of 2. If the early investors need to liquidate the stocks right away at 8 (e.g. they need the funds), they will lose actual money.

Market Efficiency and Related Issues

Investors need information to trade in the stock market. The flow of information in the market is a measure of its efficiency. Unfortunately, most markets (including our local market) are somewhat inefficient. There are certain investors that have access to information earlier. Some information may only be available to a certain group of people. These information may significantly influence stock prices. People who have access to these ahead of others may also make more money ahead of others. Some issues related to market inefficiency are insider trading, market manipulation, and fair dealing.

Insider Trading

For example, company A is a petroleum corporation. News of an oil well discovery will increase its stock price tremendously. This information will be first known to the company executives before it becomes public. The company executives can in theory buy stocks at their current prices before they release the information, which will result in a financial windfall for them.

The above practice is illegal, and is known as insider trading. The insider here does not exclusively refer to actual company insiders but to anybody who has access to the inside information. A journalist who has the exclusive scoop on the oil well discovery may trade on the information before making a news report. He will be guilty of insider trading as well. Unfortunately, the insider trading rule in the local market is very difficult to monitor and enforce.

Market Manipulation

An increase in buying will increase the price of the stock and vice versa. Usually, the demand for stocks is brought about by market forces. However, some traders might create schemes to artificially increase or decrease the price of stocks. Some traders might initiate a buying frenzy when the stock market opens to create a stock rally and sell the stocks (at now higher prices) before the market realizes that there was really nothing to back up that rally.

Some traders may even "advise" some of their clients to buy certain stocks to push their prices up (they may be doing this because they are invested in the stocks themselves, or they are in cahoots with their other clients). Smaller, less-informed clients, can unwittingly be used as pawns for market manipulation. These are all possible because the traders have better access to information than ordinary investors.

Fair Dealing

A brokerage firm may prioritize a client with a 100 million account over a client with only 100 thousand. The firm may give information and advice to the bigger clients before they tend to smaller investors. The firm may also give priority to bigger clients for IPO subscriptions before smaller clients. A firm will earn more commission per work done from a bigger account than from a smaller one. The above practices are contrary to the concept of fair dealing. Unfortunately, fair dealing is more of an ethical than a legal rule, and smaller investors may not even notice that they are being treated unfairly.

How to Invest in the Stock Market

DIRECTLY, through a licensed stock broker/ firm. The investor can order trades through his stock broker via the phone, email, or an online interactive platform.

INDIRECTLY, via a fund that invests in the stock market. Mutual, exchange traded, and index funds are examples.

Due to transaction fees and analysts' costs, investing in the stock market follows the concept of **economies of scale**. An investor with small or moderate funds might be better off investing in a fund than investing in the stock market directly.

Some Ways to Earn Money in the Stock Market

1. Through issued dividends on common stocks and fixed dividends on preferred stocks

2. By buying undervalued stocks and selling overvalued stocks

3. By shorting overvalued stocks. However, short-selling is not permitted locally

4. Through interest earned for stocks that can be or subsequently converted to bonds

5. By buying warrants that eventually result in cheaper strike than market prices when exercised

6. By selling stocks at higher than market value to entities who are hoarding shares of a certain company (e.g. either to takeover the company or to defend against a takeover); these entities are willing to buy shares at a premium

7. Indirectly, via the increase in the net asset value of funds (e.g. mutual funds) that are invested in the stock market

8. By buying stocks of distressed companies (e.g. companies on the verge of bankruptcy) in the hopes that restructuring may increase their values in the future

9. By investing in derivatives linked to the stock market (e.g. index futures)

2.2

FIXED INCOME
INVESTMENTS
(BONDS)

Financial District, Singapore

Singapore has one of the most developed bond
markets in Asia.

*"If I owe you a pound, I have a problem;
but if I owe you a million, the problem is
yours."*
- John Maynard Keynes

What are Bonds?

A lot of new investors find bonds mysterious. Bonds are actually debts. The borrower of the money is the issuer of the bond. The lender of the money is the investor in the bond.

How do debts become bonds? Suppose a company wants to borrow one million. There are not a lot of people who can, or are willing to lend the full 1,000,000, but there are easily 1,000 people who can or will lend 1,000 each.

Bonds are financial securities that represent units of debt, the same way that stocks represent units of company ownership.

Another reason why debt has to be broken up into units is for the purpose of trading (buying and selling) prior to maturity. A lender cannot easily sell 1,000,000 worth of debt to another investor. By breaking up that same debt into units, an investor can trade smaller portions of the debt. This also makes it easier to invest in debt from different borrowers; hence, lessening the risk via diversification.

Bonds that can be traded are bearer bonds, meaning whoever bears or holds the bonds (traditionally certificates; but could now just be computer records) is entitled to the payments. Therefore, an investor must check whether the bonds he is buying are negotiable/tradable.

Bond trading facilitates liquidity. If you are a holder (investor) of a ten-year bond, do you expect to see the principal only after ten years? What if you need access to your money before ten years? Bond trading allows investors to cash in on the bonds at any time they wish regardless of the tenor of the bond. If bond trading doesn't exist, long term debt will not be attractive to investors because of illiquidity.

Bond-Related Terms

The amount to be borrowed, the principal, is referred to as the **face value** or **par value**.

Debts or loans have a period at which they are pledged to be fully paid. This period is the **tenor** of the bond. Debt the borrower promises to pay in one year has a tenor of one year. **Maturity** refers to the remaining time for which the debt will be fully paid. For example, a bond with a ten year tenor seven years after issuance will mature in three years.

Bonds pay interest. The interest may be paid yearly, semi-annually (most common), or not at all during the term of the debt. This is known as the **coupon**. Coupon is expressed as the percentage of the face value that is paid in one year.

A 1,000 debt with a coupon of 10% will pay 100 in yearly interest. For the same debt, an annual coupon will pay 100 yearly, while a semi-annual coupon will pay 50 every 6 months.

Some debts will not pay regular interests. Instead, these interests will be compounded until maturity. This applies to **zero coupon** bonds.

Pricing of Bonds

At the time of issuance, coupon bonds have prices equal to their face values. Zero coupon bonds are priced differently upon issuance. The issuance price of a zero coupon bond is such that when compounded annually until maturity at the quoted interest rate, it will equal the face value.

A zero coupon 10% bond that is expected to pay out 1,000 in 5 years will be priced at 620.9 at issuance. 620.9 compounded at 10% for 5 years will amount to 1,000.

As time goes by, bonds will fluctuate in price. The fluctuation will vary with the prevailing interest rate. This is the reason why bonds have **interest rate risk**.

As prevailing interest rates increase, bonds will normally fall in price compared to the face value. Why is this so? As interest rates increase, previously issued bonds based on the old interest rates will be less attractive to investors since bond issuers will issue new bonds with higher coupons. The only way that these old bonds will sell is if they are sold at lower prices. Bonds that sell at prices lower than their face values are said to be "selling at a **discount**".

The opposite happens when interest rates decrease. Previously issued bonds based on old interest rates will be more attractive to investors since bond issuers will issue new bonds with lower coupons. These bonds will sell at higher prices. Bonds that sell at prices higher than their face values are said to be "selling at a **premium**".

When interest rates remain the same, bonds will neither sell at a discount or premium. These bonds are said to be "selling at **par**".

As bonds approach maturity, their prices will approach par and fluctuate less with interest rates. Therefore, short term bonds have less interest rate risk than longer term bonds.

Due to the fixed income nature of bonds, and the wide availability of interest rate data which makes bond pricing easy, bonds generally have less risk than stocks.

How Bonds Pay Investors

Example 1: A 5 year 5% semi-annual coupon bond with a face value of PHP 1,000 was issued. When and how much are the payments?

Answer: PHP 25 each at 6, 12, 18, 24, 30, 36, 42, 48, 54 months after issuance; PHP 1025 (last interest payment of 25 plus 1,000 principal) 60 months after issuance

Example: 2 The same bond as above, except with annual coupon. When and how much are the payments?

Answer: PHP 50 each at 12, 24, 36, 48 months after issuance; PHP 1050 60 months after issuance

Example 3: The same bond as above, but with zero coupon.

Answer: Only PHP 1000 at 60 months, there will be no other prior payments

For the examples given, the coupon bonds are priced at PHP 1,000 at issuance. The zero coupon bond is priced at only PHP 783.5 at issuance. The price of a zero coupon bond will rise to par as it matures.

In practice, bonds with tenors longer than two years are usually coupons, while those with tenors two years or shorter are usually zero coupons.

Since bonds may be sold at different prices, it may be difficult for investors to discern which bonds have the most discount or premium percentage wise. This is the reason why in financial reports, bond prices are reported relative to a 100 par value. A 1,000 par bond selling for 1,000 will be reported as priced at 100. If the same bond sells for 980, it will be reported as priced at 98. If the same bond sells for 1025, it will be reported as priced at 102.5

Returns from Bonds

With bonds, during their term, returns will come from the coupon payments. However, coupons are not the only sources of returns. If bonds are held to maturity, the differences between par and purchase prices will form part of the return. A bond may be purchased at any time after issuance. Prices after issuance may be at a premium, discount or par. A bond purchased at discount will result in additional gains at maturity.

Yield to maturity (YTM) is the most often used measure of bond return. YTM factors in coupon payments and price appreciation. YTM also assumes that the coupons are reinvested at the YTM rate.

Interest Rate Risk

When prevailing interest rates increase, bond prices fall. The opposite happens when rates decrease. The longer the bond matures, the higher the interest rate risk.

Reinvestment Risk

When coupons are paid, the investor can reinvest them. There is a risk that the investor will not find another investment that will match the coupon rate. The higher the coupon rate, the higher the reinvestment risk. Zero coupon bonds don't have this risk.

Credit Risk

Credit risk is an important source of risk for bonds so I'll discuss it in this section. Credit worthiness of an entity (whether an individual, group, corporation or government institution) is measured by that entity's **ability** and **willingness** to pay its obligations.

The more assets the entity has, the higher is its ability to pay its obligations. The higher the income of an entity, the higher is its ability to pay. These are reasons why banks, when conducting due diligence investigations for loans, check and verify potential borrowers' assets and income.

Sometimes, despite an entity's ability to pay, it may refuse to do so. Some borrowers will refuse to pay due to disagreements with the loan terms. Others will refuse to pay simply because they are dishonorable. Unlike ability, the willingness of an entity to pay is more difficult to measure. Lenders will often check the borrower's credit history to check for this, but this doesn't guarantee anything. Lenders may resort to means to compel payment. These means are often included in the loan/trade agreement.

Utility providers (water, phone, electricity) will often cut service when obligations are not paid. If the borrower wishes the service to resume, the borrower must pay a portion or all of his pending obligations.

Banks often require **collateral** to guarantee payment of loans. If the borrower wishes to retain the properties put up as collateral, the borrower must pay a portion or all of his pending obligations.

Credit card companies, which do not require collateral, will just charge borrowers with high interest rates to compensate for the high risk nature of the loans.

Investigation on a particular entity's credit worthiness is a difficult and time consuming process. Big banks may have their own credit investigation departments, but smaller lenders do not have those resources. This is where **credit score/ credit rating** agencies come in. Credit score agencies assess the credit worthiness of individuals. Credit rating agencies assess the credit worthiness of companies, governments, and their specific bond issues.

Moody's, Standard and Poor's (S&P), and **Fitch** are the "big three" credit rating agencies in the world. The importance of these agencies is practically set in stone. Interest rates for a particular bond issue rise and fall based on their ratings. Large borrowers may ask two or all of these agencies to rate their issuances.

The higher the credit rating (hence lower credit risk), the lower the interest rate demanded by investors. This is the reason why credit ratings for the Philippines by these three are always cited in the news.

Investment Grade Bonds

The big three credit agencies rate bond issues. Each agency has their own set of ratings. For S&P and Fitch, the best rating is AAA. For Moody's, the best rating is Aaa. If bonds are rated BBB- or better (for S&P and Fitch), they are considered investment grade. For Moody's, the corresponding rating is Baa3. Both BBB- and Baa3 ratings are nine grades below the highest rating.

Whether a bond issue is investment grade or not, carries a lot of significance. Some regulations restrict certain institutions to invest only in investment grade bonds. For example, some insurance companies and pension funds may only be allowed to invest in these bonds. The news of the recent upgrade of Philippine bonds to investment grade is very significant. Many investors, who were previously disallowed to invest in Philippine bonds, may now do so.

Speculative Grade Bonds

Bond issues rated below investment grade are called speculative grade bonds. Though they are also known as "junk bonds", they are by no means worthless.

Credit Spread

The difference between the yields of a lower grade bond versus a higher one is known as the credit spread. The higher yield corresponds to the higher risk of the lower rated bond.

Misconception with Bonds

1. Bonds, as investments, need to be held to maturity to recoup the principal.

   FALSE. Bonds can be sold prior to maturity to recoup the investment. However, the price may be at a discount or premium to the original principal.

2. Bonds, as investments, will NOT lose money.

   FALSE. When interest rates rise, bonds fall in value.

3. Bonds, as investments, are relatively safe since there are interest payments during the term of the bond and a principal payment at maturity.

   NOT NECESSARILY. Borrowers may not be able or willing to pay the interests and principal when due. Most common forms of bonds are not backed by collateral.

4. Bonds, as investments, perform well in a good economy.

   NOT NECESSARILY. In fact, bonds may even perform badly in a good economy. As economic activity increases, the government may increase interest rates to keep the economy from overheating and to control inflation; bond prices will fall with this move.

Types of Bonds

Treasuries – These are bonds that are issued and guaranteed by the National Treasury. Since a government, issuing a bond in its own currency, has taxing powers and can "print" money as necessary, these bonds are considered **risk-free** (at least credit risk-wise).

Treasuries issued by a country in a currency not its own (e.g. Philippine bonds in US Dollar), are called **sovereign bonds**. They are NOT risk-free and their yields depend on their credit ratings.

Treasury bills or T-Bills are those with maturities two years or less. Treasury notes mature between two and ten years. Treasury bonds mature in ten years or more.

Corporate issues – These are debts issued by corporations and other private entities. Since the coupon and principal payments depend on the ability and willingness of the corporations to pay, corporate bonds have added credit risk compared to treasuries with similar maturities. This added credit risk will be in the form of a higher interest rate.

The difference between the yields of a corporate and a treasury bond with similar maturities is the credit spread. The more credit worthy the corporation is, the lower the credit spread, and vice versa

In general, bonds with longer maturities have higher interest rates than similarly rated bonds with shorter maturities; provided both bonds are issued at (or near) the same time. The higher interest is for both the added interest rate and liquidity risks.

Bonds with Call and Put Options

Callable bonds are bonds with **call options**. With these bonds, the issuer (borrower) has the option to buy back or "call" the bonds from the investors prior to maturity.

Example: Company A issues 10-year bonds (with a par value of 100) with 5% semi-annual coupon, callable at 5 years for 102.

Callability generally gives the issuer the advantages. If prevailing interest rates fall significantly, bond prices will rise. If the "theoretical" price rises above 102 (e.g. 105), the company can opt to buy back or "call" the bonds cheaply. Also, as interest rates fall, the company may issue bonds with the new lower coupons (e.g. 3 or 4%) and "call" the older bonds to cease paying the higher interest on them.

Because of the advantages callability provides the issuer, investors will tend to choose non-callable over similar callable bonds. To counteract this, callable bonds may have higher coupons than similar non-callable bonds. They will typically be cheaper than similar non-callable bonds.

I used the word "theoretical" to describe the bond price rise because in reality, the call price will be the **ceiling price** for callable bonds.

Putable bonds are bonds with **put options**. With these bonds, the investor (lender) has the option to sell or "put" the bonds back to the issuer prior to maturity.

Example: Company B issues 10-year bonds with 5% semi-annual coupon, putable at 5 years for 100.

Putability generally gives the investor advantages. If the prevailing interest rates rise significantly, bond prices will fall. The investor can then opt to sell back or "put" the bond back to the issuer (at 100 for this bond) and avoid the loss. Also, when interest rates rise, the investor can buy new bonds with higher coupons by putting the old bonds with lower coupons. For these bonds, the put price is the **floor price**.

Because of the advantages putability provides the investor, investors will tend to choose putable over similar non-putable bonds. Putable bonds, due to the higher demand for them, are typically more expensive than similar non-putable bonds.

Companies who need to raise capital quickly, in a very competitive or not so optimal bond market, may issue putable bonds to make them more attractive to investors.

Some Ways to Earn Money with Bonds

1. Through interest paid out as coupons, or compounded interest for zero-coupon bonds

2. By buying bonds at a discount to par or by selling bonds at a premium to par

3. By buying bonds that are priced cheaper than is attributable to interest rate or credit rating changes, or by selling bonds more expensive than is attributable to interest or credit rating changes

4. For putable bonds, by selling back the bonds to the issuer at a predetermined advantageous put price

5. For convertible bonds (bonds that can be converted to common stocks) or bonds converted to common stocks in a subsequent agreement (e.g. bankruptcy); through dividends and capital appreciation of the resulting stocks

6. By buying defaulted bonds which may be sold by their original bearers very cheaply, there is a chance that the issuer may recover in the future enough to compel it (e.g. via courts) to pay its past obligations

7. Via derivatives that are linked to bonds

2.3

CASH AND CASH-LIKE INVESTMENTS

The United States Dollar

It is also the de facto cash of the world.

"Revenue is vanity... margin is sanity... cash is king"
- Anonymous

Cash as an Investment Asset Class

Bank Deposits

Savings and time deposits are cash investments. Money in an ordinary savings account can be immediately withdrawn while that in a time deposit account can only be withdrawn after a specified period. Premature withdrawal from a time deposit will incur penalties that may eat up the principal. Time deposits are not as liquid as ordinary savings accounts. Both with savings and time deposits, only the original depositors have access; hence, these deposits are not tradable.

Certificates of Deposits (CDs), on the other hand, may be traded. Tradable CDs are known as negotiable CDs. Bearers (meaning those who have possession, not necessarily the original depositors) of negotiable CDs will be able to access the deposit after the prescribed term. If Mr. A bought a 5 year negotiable CD with a face value of 100,000 and interest of 5%, he does not have to wait 5 years to access the money. Mr. A can sell the CD to another entity prior to maturity. Some CDs are priced like zero coupon bonds; meaning they are initially priced at an amount that when compounded at the interest rate for the duration of the investment, will yield the face value. Some CDs may also be structured and priced like coupon bonds; meaning they are initially priced at face value, will pay out periodic interests, and the face value can be withdrawn at maturity.

CDs may or may not be insured by the government. Philippine issued **Long Term Negotiable CDs** (LTNCD) are usually insured up to PHP 500,000.

Like bonds, CDs may fluctuate in value with regards to interest rates; Unlike bonds, CDs are issued only by banks. Bonds can be issued by any entity.

Cash-like Investments

Some short term debts are "cash-like" investments. For them to be cash-like, they must be liquid and safe. Their short term nature makes them liquid. A safe security is one with no or very minimal risk. Not all short term debts are safe. Only debts from very credit worthy borrowers qualify.

Treasury bills are short term debts from a very credit worthy borrower, which is the government. Short term corporate debts from very credit worthy companies also qualify as safe. Unsecured debt securities issued by these companies, with terms 270 days or less, are known as **commercial paper**.

Cash, negotiable certificates of deposits, treasury bills, and commercial paper, all trade in what is known as the **money market**.

Purpose of Cash/ Cash-like Investments

The two reasons for investing in cash/ cash-like investments are liquidity and safety.

When an investor has spending needs in the short term, he needs to put his money where it can easily be taken out. Short term usually refers to a period of one year or less. Cash and cash like investments are very stable with regards to their value, which makes them safe. Unlike with stocks that may significantly fluctuate in value even within minutes, cash investments maintain their value over the short term. If ever there will be fluctuations with their principal (such as with CDs or short term debt), these will be minimal. Since short term debts traded in the money market involve only issues from very credit worthy sources, safety is almost guaranteed.

Cash Investments and Conservatism

Very conservative investors prefer cash investments. It is not uncommon to see some high net worth individuals put most of their money in deposits.

In the Philippines, many investors have been spoiled by the prevalence of high-interest time deposit accounts decades ago. Five-year "double your money" time deposits were still being offered as recent as ten years ago. As per the rule of 72, the interest on these accounts was around 14.4% annually.

In today's investment climate, these high rates are no longer feasible. Currently, banks in the Philippines offer time deposits with yields of around 1%. Still, many investors hold on to the mentality of putting most of their money in cash.

This mentality may be attributed to **loss aversion**. They would rather forgo potential larger gains from riskier investments than lose a portion of their money.

A big challenge for financial advisers is to convince their conservative clients to invest in riskier investments instead of just cash. The problem is that if the risky investments lose some money in the short term, the financial advisers get the blame.

Cash Investments, Inflation, and Opportunity Costs

Investors who place their money on cash instruments think that they aren't losing money. However, cash investments bear inflation and opportunity costs. Due to inflation, money loses purchasing power over time. The yield in cash investments is usually less than the inflation rate. Over many years, money kept in deposits will lose significant purchasing power.

When investors put their money in cash investments, they miss out on potential gains that they may have earned have they placed their money in riskier assets. These are the costs of opportunity.

2.4

MUTUAL FUNDS

Roll the dice - *to assume a risk by taking action*

Mutual funds allow investors to roll with plenty of
dice in one go.

*"The best argument for mutual funds is that
they offer safety and diversification. But they
don't necessarily offer safety and
diversification. "*
- Ron Chernow

What is a Mutual Fund?

A mutual fund is not a separate investment class; rather it is a pooled investment of any, or a combination of (usually traditional) assets or asset classes.

What are the ADVANTAGES of investing in mutual funds vs. creating your own portfolio?

Economies of Scale

Buying one gallon of ice cream is cheaper than buying eight individual pints. Economies of scale refers to how items become cheaper per unit when bought at higher volumes. Buying securities also works that way. Transaction costs become cheaper per security when trading at higher volumes. Mutual funds trade securities at high volumes. An investor, trading on his own, will incur higher per unit costs. Associated costs, such as for research and asset management, will be cheaper for a mutual fund because of the larger scale.

Lower Cost of Entry

In creating your own stock portfolio, you may need a large amount upfront. With mutual funds, you can start investing by buying a small portion of the fund that holds the stock portfolio. Locally, some mutual funds have entry costs as low as PHP 10,000.

Ease of Diversification

Diversification is key in lowering investment risk. Investing in mutual funds allows you to invest in an already diversified portfolio. Of course, you can invest in a diversified portfolio by yourself, but that comes with higher costs of entry, and higher per unit costs due to the small scale.

What are the DISADVANTAGES of investing in mutual funds vs. creating your own portfolio?

Higher Cash Holdings

Mutual funds need to maintain significant portions of their portfolio in cash to accommodate withdrawals. Since cash has much lower expected returns than bonds or stocks, the overall returns of mutual funds will be reduced.

Difficulty in Comparing One Fund from Another

Mutual funds with similar strategies may differ in composition. The actual composition of these portfolios may not always be available to potential investors. Mutual funds will have several assets in their portfolios. It is therefore difficult for an individual investor to process all these information in choosing a fund. Some investors may be forced to evaluate funds based on past performance, which may not be reliable in predicting future performance.

Lack of Control

The fund managers control the execution of the investment strategy, not the investor.

Lack of Specification and Adaptability

Mutual funds already have set investment strategies and you pick those funds that have strategies that resemble your own. It's like buying ready to wear clothing, the funds may approximate your "fit", but it may not fit you perfectly. A fund that closely fits your investment profile may not even exist. More importantly, once set, the strategy of a fund will not change. If your investment profile changes significantly, the fund will not adapt to you. If this happens, you may have to withdraw from the fund and bear the associated penalties.

High Associated Costs

Some funds may have high **front-load** costs (fees you have to pay upon investment), management fees, and premature withdrawal penalties.

Asymmetrical Performance Fees

Some fund managers will get a percentage of your earnings when your investments increase in value, but they may not share in your losses when they devaluate. For example, a mutual fund with a performance fee of 2% will charge you PHP 2 for every PHP 100 you gain.

If your share in the fund earns 100,000, the fund managers will get a 2,000 cut. If your share in the fund loses 100,000, nobody owes you anything. This will encourage the fund manager to take more than the appropriate risk, since he will share only in the gains but not in the losses.

Depending on the terms of the fund, the fund may charge you performance fees for actual non-performance. For example, last year, your share in the fund lost 100,000. This year, your share in the fund earned 100,000 from last year; therefore you will be charged 2,000 this year. However, your losses and gains for the two years canceled each other out resulting in actual zero profit; but you were charged 2,000 for the "gains" in the second year.

Types of Mutual Funds

Money Market Funds - These are funds invested in short term, low risk securities, such as treasury bills, certificate of deposits, and high grade commercial paper. These are for investors who want safety and liquidity for their portfolios. Securities in these funds are those discussed under cash and cash-like investments.

Fixed Income or Bond Funds – The funds may be composed of treasuries, corporate bonds, sovereigns, or a combination of any or all.

Unlike the bonds procured for money market funds, bonds for fixed income funds have longer terms. They may include high risk bonds.

Equity Funds – These are funds that invest in stocks. The funds may focus on particular stocks with regards to capitalization; large market capitalization (large cap), small (small cap), or those in between (mid cap). The funds may also focus on growth, value, or a blend of both stock types. The funds may also mimic the components and proportions of an index. These are known as **index funds.** There are index funds that mimic or **track** the DJIA, S&P 500, NASDAQ, etc.

Balanced Funds – These are funds that combine two or more asset classes. The aim of these funds is better diversification.

An investor may also hold a variety of mutual fund types in his portfolio.

The funds can be denominated in local or foreign currency (e.g. dollar fund). Since companies assign proprietary names to their funds, it may be confusing for an investor to identify which funds are which types.

Insurance Plans as Investments

A lot of insurance companies are now marketing insurance plans as investments. These investments usually involve mutual funds so I'll be discussing them in this section.

Insurance is a **risk protection strategy**. There are events that occur very infrequently, but when they do, they cause tremendous financial losses. For these types of risks, insurance is a good risk management strategy.

Fire is an unlikely occurrence for most property owners, but when this occurs, the owner is often stuck with significant financial losses (damage to structure, furniture and other valuables).The property owner buys an insurance policy to cover for these losses.

When death occurs, the deceased is deprived of his future earnings. A dead person can't work and earn money; and therefore can no longer provide support for his dependents. To protect against loss of future earning capacity, a person can take out a life insurance policy so that his dependents will not suffer financially due to his death. The same can be said about permanent disability, since the disabled will be deprived of future earnings.

There are insurance policies that also cover for sickness, car accident, theft, etc.

Insurance companies practice **risk pooling**. The chance of a single life policy holder dying within the year may be significant, but the chance of thousands of life policy holders all dying together within the year is much much less. The same goes for health insurance. The chance of a single policy holder getting hospitalized may be significant, but the chance of thousands of policy holders all being hospitalized within the same period is very very small.

When an event occurs (either death or hospitalization as per the examples), the claim is paid out from the pooled premiums of all the policy holders. The chance that many members will experience the event within the same period is highly unlikely. This ensures that the insurance companies will not be paying out claims en-masse and go bankrupt. This is the reason why certain catastrophic events that affect a lot of people such as "acts of God" or nuclear war are not covered, since most policy holders will suffer the events at the same time. Some policy holders will probably never even experience the event they're insuring against during the covered term.

Life insurance is also a very popular **estate planning strategy**. Payouts from life insurance policies are exempted from estate taxes. The payouts also provide liquidity to the dependents to pay for estate taxes, funeral expenses, etc. Another important advantage of life insurance in estate planning is that the claims do not have to go through **probate**.

Probate is a process in which the court administers a deceased person's estate and distribute it to heirs. Even the last will and testament can be contested, but a life insurance policy cannot be. Creditors of the deceased can have a claim on the deceased's estate but they have none on the life insurance paid out to the beneficiaries.

As a buyer of an insurance policy, you should be aware that the premium you pay goes into a pooled fund that is used to pay other policy holders when they make claims. The insurance company can invest the fund to grow it, but they are mandated by government regulators to invest it in low risk investments (mostly bonds). If there are excess funds, referring to assets that exceed projected payouts; those are the only funds they can place in moderate risk investments such as equities. Even then, gains from those may be used to pay the company's expenses, or may end up as the insurer's profits. The policy holder doesn't have money that can be separated from the pooled fund. To access the fund, the policy holder needs to experience the untoward event; but not all holders will experience the event during the covered term. In fact, only few of them will. That's how insurance is designed.

Insurance companies now sell **Variable Life Insurance (VLI)**, an insurance plan combined with an investment fund. The insurers market this as a "2 for 1" scheme and many investors are swayed. However, a VLI is actually a "2 for 2" scheme, and probably worse.

Most of the money one puts in will be treated as premiums and will go into the "risk pool" as described previously. Only a small portion will go into a managed fund (just like a mutual fund).

If one buys into a VLI and the monthly payment is 4,000, while a stand-alone insurance policy (similar to what is included in the VLI) costs 3,000 monthly, then only 1,000 will be placed in a managed fund. The portion placed in the managed fund may even be less if the pooled fund used to pay for insurance claims suffers a shortfall. Money from the managed fund may be used to plug that.

One can potentially earn more if one places the whole 4,000 in a mutual fund instead of a VLI. The insurance companies may charge additional fees if fund management is outsourced.

Since a large portion of one's VLI contributions is tied to the pooled risk fund (as I mentioned, a holder's share cannot be separated from the pool), withdrawing the contributions will be difficult. The insurer may allow the withdrawal, but it will come with significant pretermination penalties.

As with stand-alone insurance policies, if the VLI holder becomes remiss in his payments, the VLI may be voided and most contributions may be forfeited.

Disadvantages of Variable Life Insurance vs. a Stand Alone Mutual Fund

1. A large portion of the contributions are set aside as life insurance premiums, the remainder is placed in the investment fund. If the insurer has a funding shortfall from claims, the money from the managed fund may be diverted to the insurance fund. In a mutual fund, all the contributions are invested.

2. The investor is required to make regular monthly contributions (to fund the premium portion), failing to do so may result in forfeiture. In a mutual fund, the investor is not required to make contributions after the initial investments.

3. If the insurance company is outsourcing management of the managed fund, the company may charge higher fees than what a stand-alone fund charges.

4. The investor in a VLI needs to hold the investment for a very long period (mainly due to the insurance component), and pretermination will incur large penalties. Mutual funds also have mandated minimum holding periods (usually one year) but they are much shorter than what insurers require. Premature withdrawal fees of mutual funds are much less.

5. The managed fund portion of the VLI may have less versatility with regards to investment strategy because of the ties to the risk pool fund and its long term nature. Sure, you may set the strategy at the beginning, but it may be cumbersome to change strategies once your financial profile changes. With mutual funds, you can choose a fund that fits your investment strategy and shift to another fund as needed.

6. Most importantly, unlike mutual fund shares, VLIs are not negotiable securities.

The obvious advantage (and selling point) of a VLI is the actual life policy itself, but you are better off buying a separate stand alone term life policy if you actually need one. VLIs may also enjoy tax advantages.

If you have no dependents, getting life insurance is not necessary since no one needs to be protected from financial losses with your death. It is not uncommon for insurance agents to ask parents to buy VLI policies for their children. This is absurd since children do not have financial dependents of their own.

Some insurance companies now offer stand alone mutual fund accounts. This may be the better option compared to getting a VLI from them; but then again, a lot of non-insurance institutions specialize in mutual fund products.

2.5

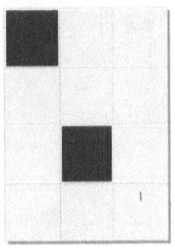

ALTERNATIVE
INVESTMENTS

A Housing Bubble... Literally!

Overspeculation on real estate may lead to housing
market bubbles

*"It's not whether you're right or wrong
that's important, but how much money you
make when you're right and how much you
lose when you're wrong."*
- George Soros

Real Estate

Most investors are familiar with this asset class.

Advantages of Real Estate as an Investment

1. Real Estate (RE) is tangible, and investors value assets that they can see and feel.

2. Since RE is tangible, it is something that investors can utilize themselves or can rent out.

3. Each RE property is unique, which a seller can exploit in setting prices.

4. RE is an investment class than many people understand since a lot of people own property.

5. RE correlates well with inflation since housing prices are major determinants of the inflation index. As general prices go up, the prices of real estate go up as well.

Disadvantages of Real Estate as an Investment

1. RE is subject to periodic expenses such as maintenance costs, real estate taxes, utility costs, security, financing costs, etc. For many investors without consistent rental income, the above may result in significant negative cash flow.

2.   RE has low liquidity. Because most RE cost million (in PHP), they are not easy to buy and sell. The investor may need to reduce the selling price or pay broker commissions, in order to facilitate liquidity.

3.   Since each RE is unique, RE is difficult to value. The illiquidity also adds to this difficulty.

4.   RE tends to be an emotional investment. An investor may tend to make irrational decisions with his RE assets (e.g. overpricing, reluctance to sell, etc.)

Investors now have the option to invest in shares of funds that are invested in real estate properties. These are known as REIT or **Real Estate Investment Trusts**. Since the shares only represent a small fraction of the value of the actual properties, these shares are easier to trade; hence the high liquidity.

A REIT corporation is formed with real estate assets under its name. The shares of the REIT corporation can then trade in the stock market. However, in the Philippines, the launch of REIT trading has been stalled by issues related to taxation and minimum public ownership.

Private Equity

This refers to investment in equities which are not listed in the stock market. Most companies are not listed in the stock market.

Advantages of Investing in Private Equity

1. Stocks in newly established companies are priced cheaply. As the company earns revenues and grows, the stocks may have significant appreciation. The returns can be many times the original investments.

2. If investing in a company when shares are at their cheapest, and interested investors are few (such as with distressed companies); an investor may buy a significant number of shares, enough to influence or even control management.

3. It is easier to find bargains due to lack of market-driven price discovery.   Discounts for lack of liquidity can also be had.

Disadvantages of Investing in Private Equity

1. Since private equity is not traded in the stock market, it has low liquidity.

2. Private equity requires long term commitment of funds. Despite this, there is no guarantee that the investor will see returns.

3. Private equities' fair market values are not readily available and will require financial analysts to compute for them.

4.   Many startup companies fail, and even fewer grow big enough to reach IPO stage.

5.   Transactions involving private equity will incur the usual capital gains and documentary stamp taxes.

6.   Some companies (e.g. distressed or bankrupt) may be embroiled in legal issues involving their assets and ownership.

Some Ways to Earn from Private Equity

1. Dividends, if any, paid out by the company

2. Proceeds from the sale of a portion or the whole company

3. When the company goes public in an IPO, the investor can sell his shares in the stock market

4. Proceeds from sales of stocks to interested buyers - Despite being not traded in the stock market, shares in private companies may be bought by interested parties

Antiques, Art, Collectibles

A lot of people buy art pieces as investments. Some pieces from popular and renowned artists fetch high prices on the market. The investor who initially bought these pieces when the artists were unknown or the market demand for the artworks were less, will earn handsome returns.

There are many other items that increase in value through time. Comic books, toys, watches, cars, stamps, coins and handbags are some examples.

These collectibles often have high associated costs. These articles must be maintained at mint condition to keep their values. Security and insurance are also musts for very valuable items. The above refers to **holding costs**.

When the items are put up for sale, the owners may need to pay for independent experts to authenticate the items. When the items are eventually sold, auction houses and sales agents often get a big share of the proceeds.

The big risk here for investors is picking the inexpensive items that will end up being valuable. Many investors might end up with something unsellable. A collector may also overpay for something and eventually sell it at a loss. Expensive art and collectibles have limited market bases. Market demand may not be that strong during economic downturns.

Commodities

Crude oil, gold, corn are some of the commodities that trade in major exchanges around the world. Entities that will actually use these commodities (e.g. petroleum companies using crude oil), may buy such items in current time (spot transaction) and take delivery of such items. End users may also buy derivatives (forward, future and option contracts) on these commodities, in hopes of locking in advantageous prices.

There are many investors who go into commodities trading for purely speculative reasons, and will not actually need the commodities for business or personal purposes. A speculator need not have a place in his house to store barrels of oil or bushels of corn. Speculative commodities transactions involve cash settlement (for gains and losses), and do not require actual physical possession or delivery of commodities.

Though speculation has been blamed for driving commodity prices up, it actually plays a vital role in price discovery. For speculators, the futures market is the best place for "pure-play" on commodities. However, there is no futures market in the Philippines since derivatives trading is not yet allowed.

Though a lot of money can be made with commodities, it is quite easy to lose money as well. This is due to the highly leveraged and high risk nature of commodities transactions.

Foreign Exchange

Companies which transact with foreign countries need to engage in currency trading. People who travel or work abroad have the need to buy and sell foreign currency. However, there is a large number of investors who just speculate on currency movements. Currency trading platforms are popping up everywhere, which make it easy for ordinary investors to trade.

Currency prices are expressed in pairs, with one currency as the **base** (with a fixed value of 1), and the other currency as the **quoted currency** (with a value relative to the base).

A forex quote of USD/PHP = 44.00, or USD:PHP = 44.00, or USDPHP = 44.00 means that every 1 unit of USD (US Dollar) is equal to 44 units of PHP (Philippine Peso). The first currency stated is the base currency. In this example, USD is the base currency, while PHP is the quoted currency.

Currency pairs are often quoted in two prices, the ask and bid quotes. The **ask quote** is the price the traders are willing to sell the base currency in terms of the quoted currency. The **bid quote** is the price the traders are willing to buy the base currency in terms of the quoted currency. The midpoints of the ask and bid quotes are often the values shown in television or written in newspapers. The difference between the ask and bid quotes is the **spread**.

Example 1: For a given bank, the ask or SELL quote is USD/PHP = 44.50 while the bid or BUY quote is USD/PHP = 43.50.

This means that the bank will sell you 1 USD in exchange for 44.50 PHP (or alternatively you will be buying 1 USD from the bank with 44.50 PHP). The bank will buy from you 1 USD for 43.50 PHP (or alternatively you will sell 1 USD to the bank for 43.50 PHP). The midquote is USD/PHP = 44.00.

Example 2: There are two individuals, Mr. Tourist (T) and Mr. OFW (O). Mr. T will travel to the United States and will be spending USD. Mr. O will return to the Philippines and will be bringing home USD. Which quotes will Mr. T and Mr. O be interested in?

Mr. T will need to buy USD from the bank. Since the bank will be selling USD to Mr. T, the quote used will be the ASK or SELL price. Mr. O will be selling his USD upon coming home. Since the bank will be buying USD from Mr O, the quote used will be the BID or BUY price.

Mr T and Mr. O need not transact directly with banks. They can exchange their money in other currency exchange facilities. Notice that in our example, the ask and bid quotes differ by 1 PHP. This difference or spread is the fee of the exchanging facility since they don't charge a separate transaction fee.

The quotes and spreads vary between different exchanges. A mall exchange kiosk might have an ask quote of USD/PHP = 45.00 and a bid quote of USD/PHP = 43.00, resulting in a wider spread. An interbank currency exchange might have an ask quote of USD/PHP = 44.25 and a bid quote of USD/PHP = 43.75, resulting in a narrower spread.

Transactions between parties with high volumes (e.g. between two banks) have narrow spreads. The opposite is true for low volume transactions (e.g. between a bank and a person). These relate spread with liquidity. The higher the liquidity, the narrower the spread.

Transactions involving physical money (notes) often have wider spreads compared to electronic money (e.g. money transferred via telegraphic means).

The spread, being a transaction fee, may vary with the level of competition between exchanges. Airport exchanges often quote very wide spreads, since travelers who have urgent need for currency have not much choice in airports. The opposite is true for exchanges in busy tourist shopping districts.

The more liquid the trading between two currencies, the narrower the spread. For example, USD and PHP; with ask USD/PHP = 44.50; and bid USD/PHP = 43.50, have a spread of 1 or 2.27% of the midquote (1/44.00).

Let's look at THB (Thai Baht) vs. PHP, with ask THB/PHP = 1.50, and bid = THB/PHP = 1.30, have a spread of 0.2 or 14.29% (0.2/1.4). The spread between THB and PHP is wider because the trading between them is less liquid than that of USD and PHP.

Trading between two currencies may be indirect via an intermediary currency. Because of the wide spread between THB and PHP, it may be wiser to trade PHP to USD then USD to THB, since currency trading that involves USD would be more liquid.

Example: A Filipino wants to buy 10,000 THB for his upcoming travel. In this case, let us assume the following quotes:

USD/PHP ask = 44.50; bid = 43.50
USD/THB ask = 31.80; bid = 31.00
THB/PHP ask = 1.50; bid = 1.30

Option A: He will buy 10,000 THB at the ask quote of THB/PHP = 1.50. He will need to pay PHP 15,000.

Option B: He will buy X number of USD at the ask quote of USD/PHP = 44.50. He will sell that X number of USD at the bid quote USD/THB = 31.00 to acquire 10,000 THB. He will need to buy 322.58 USD and it will cost him just PHP 14,354.84

By direct trading, the Filipino will pay PHP 15,000, versus only PHP 14,354.84 via the other option. That's a saving of 4.30% over direct trading. The saving is attributable to the narrower spreads when trading via a more liquid intermediary currency.

Differences Between the Forex and Stock Markets:

1. Forex trading is not centralized unlike the stock market.
2. Because of decentralized trading, forex often have different quotes among different trading markets. Stock market prices are similar since there is one centralized market for any given stock.
3. The transaction fees for forex are the spreads. For stocks, there is a separate transaction fee.
4. Forex trading is open 24 hours daily while stocks trading happens only a few hours daily.
5. The forex market is not as regulated as the stock market making inexperienced investors in forex vulnerable to scams.
6. Forex trading can involve very high leverages (you can trade as much as fifty times the amount you actually have). This can result in high gains or high losses.
7. Price movements in forex are much harder to predict than with stocks.
8. Forex trading is a zero sum game; meaning in one trade, one party gains and another one loses. In a stock market rally, there will be more gainers than losers.

3

STEPS IN INVESTING

In financial planning, a calculator and pen
will come in handy. A financial planning
software or app will probably make the task
easier.

*"An investment said to have an 80% chance
of success sounds far more attractive than
one with a 20% chance of failure. The mind
can't easily recognize that they are the
same. "*
- Daniel Kahneman

STEP 1.   Make an inventory of your personal assets, liabilities, income, and expenses.

Everything you have, owe, earn, spend, are part of your financial profile. You will need to be aware of your financial profile to know if you can invest, and on how you'll invest. It seems to be an obvious step, yet a lot of people are not fully aware of their complete financial picture. Many don't even keep track of their expenses.

STEP 2. Determine if you have investible funds.

One cannot invest if one has no funds to invest with. A person earning 50,000 (the amounts from this point on will be all in PHP) but spending 60,000 will have no available funds for investment. Some borrow to invest, but the expected return from the investment should exceed the interest on the loan.

Example: Mr. A received a 10,000 bonus. He has 10,000 overdue credit card debt. His income and expenses match, more or less. Does he have investible funds?

The answer here depends on whether the person can invest the bonus on an investment that will earn more than the interest on the card debt. Credit card debt accrues interest of 30% or more   annually (excluding additional late charges). Unless the person finds an investment that earns more than that (which is unlikely), he is better off paying his credit card debt first.

STEP 3.   Determine your return and risk objectives.

Return Objective

As an investor, what is your return objective? Return refers to the amount or percentage (from the original investment amount) that you want to earn. Everyone naturally wants very high returns, but that is not realistic. High return objectives would need investments with high risks as well.

The following are examples of objectives:

- to buy something (property, vehicle, jewelry, etc.)

- to pay for the education of their children

- to have enough money for retirement

Example 1: To buy something

Mr. B, an employee, would like to buy a car in three years. He earns 50,000 (net of taxes) a month, with expenses of about 37,000. He sets aside 3,000 for his emergency fund, so he has about 10,000 monthly to invest with. He plans to save 500,000 to buy a recent model second hand vehicle in three years. Given the hassles of car loans and their accompanying high interest rates, he wishes to be able to make that purchase in cash. What is his return objective?

Amount that needs to be raised = 500,000
Time frame = three years or 36 months
Monthly contribution to investments = 10,000
Return (in percentage) to achieve that = ?

If Mr. B puts 10,000 monthly under his mattress, he will only come up with 360,000 in three years. He needs to earn 140,000 more.

The following is the INCORRECT way to compute the return objective (but many people will tend to compute it this way):

500,000/360,000 - 1 = 39%
39% / 3 years = 13% per year or 1.0833% a month

The above equation is INCORRECT since Mr. B does not have 360,000 at the start of his investment horizon. In fact, his investment contributions will only reach 360,000 at the END of the investment period. This means that Mr. B's investment should earn much more than 13% a year. At a rate of return of 1.0833% a month (derived from 13% yearly return), with 10,000 going into the fund monthly, Mr. B will only be able to make 437,431 in 36 months.

I will not show the detailed computations but a good financial analyst armed with a good financial calculator or software should be able to do the computations for you.

The CORRECT monthly rate of return needed by Mr. B is 1.796% a month (or around 21.55% per annum). A fund with a 10,000 monthly contribution which earns 21.55% annually will earn around 500,007 in 36 months.

But wait, we still have taxes to consider. Mr. B needs to earn 1.80% monthly, net of taxes. Different investments are treated differently here in the Philippines, so for the sake of simplicity, let us assume that Mr. B will invest in an interest bearing asset. Gains from this are taxed at 20%.

Considering taxes, Mr. B needs to earn 1.796%/(1- 20%) or 2.245% monthly; about 26.94% annually.

An annual return of 27% is high and the risk that needs to be taken to achieve that must be high as well. Unfortunately, Mr. B may not have the ability or willingness to tolerate losses given that his time horizon is only three years.

A good investment adviser will tell Mr. B that raising 500,000 in a manner described above may not be feasible. Mr. B may be better off settling for a lower target amount. A more conservative (but still considered high in today's investment environment) annual return of 8% (net of taxes) will earn him 405,355. Mr. B can also be advised to increase his monthly contributions. Assuming an annual return of 8% (net of taxes), Mr. B needs to increase his contributions to around 12,335 monthly to earn the 500,000 in three years.

Example 2: To pay for a child's education

Mr. F wants to set aside money for his baby (Baby B, currently at 1 year old), to fund his college education. He expects the child to start college at 18 years old. The yearly tuition fee is currently 100,000. Baby B is expected to take a four year course. Mr. F will put monthly contributions in an investment fund which pays 6% annual return (net of taxes). He will stop the contributions once Baby B starts college and he'll withdraw the required yearly tuition from the fund.

First of all, it will be INCORRECT to assume that Baby B will be needing 400,000 in total tuition fees. We have to consider inflation.

Assuming that tuition fees will rise 4% a year, the following are the CORRECT expected tuition fees 17 years from now:

1st year = 194,790
2nd year = 202,582
3rd year = 210,685
4th year = 219,112

It is INCORRECT to assume that the total money needed when Baby B starts college is the total of all inflation adjusted tuition fees which is 827,169. The reason why it is incorrect is that the money will NOT be withdrawn from the fund all at once. Only the yearly tuition fee will be withdrawn. The balance will still earn the annual rate of 6%.

The amount needed at age 18 will be less than 827,169. The 2nd year tuition (due at Year 19) is 202,582. However, its Year 18 value will be reduced by 6% (discounting the annual investment return). The 3rd year tuition (due at Year 20) needs to be discounted by six percent to determine its value for Year 19, and another 6% to determine its value for Year 18. The calculations are similar for the 4th year fees.

Here are the Year 18 values of the annual tuition fees of Baby B:

1st year = 194,790
2nd year = 191,115
3rd Year = 187,509
4th year = 183,971

The total Year 18 value of all the tuition fees is 757,385. This is much less than the 827,169 if the fees were just totaled.

Mr. F therefore needs to raise 757,385 in 17 years or 204 months. Since the annual return (net of taxes) is 6%, the monthly contribution is NOT 757,385/204 or 3,712.67. Remember that the monthly contributions will earn 6% (quoted annual rate) once invested, so the contributions will be much less.

The CORRECT amount that Mr. F needs to put in the fund is 2,144.16 monthly (fixed). The contributions will amount to 757,384 after 17 years, if placed in a fund earning 6% (net of tax) annual interest.

Example 3: To have enough money for retirement.

Mr. Y is 28 years old. He wants to retire when he reaches 65. Mr. Y expects to spend 50,000 (at current prices) monthly during retirement. He expects to live by age 85. Inflation is expected at 4% a year. He'll invest his money in a fund that is expected to make 7% annually (net of taxes) in the long term. How much money will Mr. Y need at retirement?

This is probably the most common reason for investing. This is because in retirement, a person will probably no longer have any regular income, so the investment is expected to fund that person's expenses.

The 50,000 at today's prices (Year 28) will be worth 213,404.49 when he turns 65, based on an annual inflation rate of 4%.

Upon retirement, his monthly expenses will grow at the rate of inflation as well. However, he will only withdraw his monthly expenses from the fund when due and the balance will remain in the fund and still earn returns.

The computations will follow a pattern similar to the one for the tuition fees, but it will be much more complicated because our expenses are monthly and the spending period is 20 years.

If Mr. Y lives until age 85, he will spend 78,271,353. As you can see, I didn't just multiply 213,404.49 by 240 months to come up with 51,217,078; this is INCORRECT since it does not account for inflation.

Does this mean that Mr. Y needs to have an investment fund balance of 78,271,353 at age 65? NO, as with my computations regarding tuition fees; upon retirement, Mr Y will not spend his fund all at once. He will only withdraw an amount (the inflation adjusted value of 50,000 in today's prices) and the balance will remain invested at 7% annually (net of taxes).

I will not show the detailed computations as with the tuition fee example.

The 78,271,353 that Mr. Y would have spent at age 85 will only need a startup value of 39,237,717.11 on retirement. The amount of 39,237,717.11 will be depleted by 213,404.49 for the first month of retirement. The next monthly payouts will increase based on an annual inflation rate of 4%. The remaining balance will have investment gains of 7% annually. After 20 years or 240 monthly payouts (when Mr. Y expects to pass away), the retirement fund will be fully depleted.

Of course, if Mr. Y spends less than projected, the retirement fund will have a balance even after age 85. If Mr. Y had already died, the remaining amount will be available for his heirs.

If Mr. Y spends more than projected, or the fund earns less than expected, the retirement fund will not last until age 85; and he will outlive his retirement fund. The danger that an investor will outlive his retirement fund is known as **longevity risk**.

To raise 39,237,717.11 at age 65, Mr. Y will have to contribute 18,715.42 monthly (fixed) to his retirement fund starting now.

Note that in the examples for tuition and retirement, I already plugged in a set return objective rather than make the return objective the unknown to be computed for. It is easier to make financial projections this way. Projections for varying return objectives can be made. Computations for more conservative (e.g. 4%) or aggressive (e.g. 10%) return objectives can be made to come up with a range of monthly contributions.

In the retirement example, take note that I used a common return objective for the periods before and during retirement for the sake of simplicity. In reality, the return objective should be lowered during retirement since a retiree is no longer able to take high risks in his investments. In fact, as retirement progresses, a retiree should invest in progressively safer and more liquid assets. As with all our examples, we assumed a net of tax return objective since it will be too complicated to account for the differences in taxation of different asset classes.

Risk Objective

Based on the concept of the return-risk trade-off; the higher the risk, the higher the potential return. An investor who takes high risks may realize high returns. He may also earn nothing or even realize high losses. An investor who takes low risks will less likely earn high returns. The low risk investor will also less likely realize high losses.

As an investor, if you tell your advisor that you don't want to lose money, your advisor may have to match you with low risk investments. Your adviser will have to explain outcomes associated with low risk investing. The reverse is true. If you tell your advisor that in the pursuit of high returns, losing money is an acceptable outcome, then your advisor will match you with high risk investments.

For some investors, what they tell their financial advisers about their willingness to take risks may not be congruent with what their actual attitudes toward risks are. For example, an investor who says he has low risk tolerance, but gambles habitually, may actually have high risk tolerance. It is up to the adviser to pick up these mixed messages and explain to the investor what his attitude towards risks really is.

The investor's **willingness** is just one component of his risk tolerance. The other component is **ability**.

What determines the ability of the individual to tolerate risk? Here are some examples.

The higher the available funds, the higher the ability to tolerate risk.

Example 1: Ms. S earns 50,000 monthly. She actually spends more than that. Proof is her unpaid credit card balance of 150,000. She has LOW ability to tolerate risk.

Example 2: Ms. F earns 100,000 monthly. She spends about 30,000 monthly. She has no outstanding debts. She has HIGH ability to tolerate risk

Example 3: Ms. L lives a frugal lifestyle. She just inherited 10 million from a distant uncle. She has HIGH ability to tolerate risk.

The higher the available funds, the higher the chance for the investor to weather losses; hence the higher tolerance for risk. The investor will also have available funds to start investing again if a previous investment went bust.

The younger the investor, the higher the ability to tolerate risk

Example 1: Mr. Y is 28 years old. He plans to invest now to fund his retirement. He will retire at age 65. He has HIGH ability to tolerate risk.

A young investor has the ability to take risk because of his longer investment horizon. In case of losses, a young investor will still have time to regain the money lost.

A young person will also have higher earning potential because of the longer period for which he will be able to work. An older person has less years to work, or may already be retired.

Example 2: Mr. Y is 28 years old. He plans to invest his money to buy a house in three years. He has LOW ability to tolerate risk.

Despite his youth, a person with a short investment horizon, or with high liquidity needs, will still have low ability. This will be discussed more in the section about constraints.

The more stable the income, the higher the ability to tolerate risk.

Example 1: Mr. B is an executive in a multinational company. He earns 300,000 monthly. He has security of tenure. He has HIGH ability to tolerate risk.

Example 2: Mr. S is an actor. He has a supporting role in a TV drama. His talent fee is a lot less than the lead actors. The show might get canceled if it does not do well in the ratings. He has LOW ability to tolerate risk.

A stabler income stream would mean that the investor can easily project his expenses and savings. The low variability (low fluctuation) of income and investible funds will enable the investor to take higher risks.

The more knowledgeable the investor is about investments, the higher the ability to tolerate risk.

Example: Mr. C works as an investment analyst. He has HIGH ability to tolerate risk.

An individual who understands what he is investing in can take higher risks.

What happens if ability and willingness don't match? What if one has high ability but low willingness to take risk? In this case, an adviser would have to educate the investor on the advantages and disadvantages of moderate and high risk investments. Hopefully, the investor will be convinced to take risks that match his ability. On the other hand, if the ability is low, but willingness is high; the investor has to temper his attitude and pick low risk investments.

Because ability is a more objective measure than willingness, the investor should base his investment decisions more towards ability when the two don't jive. However, in reality, most investors, specially those who don't have advisers, wrongly lean towards willingness.

STEP 4.   Identify and evaluate investment constraints.

In making investment decisions, the following are important factors to consider:

> Time Horizon
> Liquidity Constraints
> Legal Constraints
> Tax Considerations
> Unique Circumstances

Time Horizon

Time horizon influences risk tolerance. The specific time horizon may also determine which investments to participate in. An investor who has a very short time horizon may invest in money market funds. An investor with a long time horizon may invest in long term bonds, stocks, and real estate.

An investor's time horizon may be divided into several stages. Each stage may correspond to a different investment strategy.

Example 1: Mr. Y, 27 years old, works for a pharmaceutical company. He plans to retire at age 65.

Mr. Y has a two-stage investment horizon. The first stage is from now until he retires. The second stage will start from retirement.

Example 2: Mr. Y, 28, got married to Ms. X and had a child. The child is expected to finish school at age 22, and is expected to become financially independent thereafter. Mr. Y plans to retire at age 65.

Mr. Y now has a three-stage investment horizon. The first stage is from now until the child finishes school. The second stage is from that point until retirement. Third stage is from retirement onwards.

Liquidity Constraints

An investor has to consider his liquidity requirements in choosing investment vehicles. If the investor has expenses in the near future, which may prompt him to liquidate a portion or all of his investment, he should choose liquid assets. If an investor will have no foreseeable use of his funds in the short term, he can invest in instruments that are less liquid.

A person with spending needs that exceed his income may not even be able to invest at all.

Lack of liquidity is a form of risk. For similar investments, the less liquid investment is the riskier one.

Legal Constraints

This refers to any law, or any legally binding or enforceable agreement, that may affect investment decisions.

Example 1: A trust fund was set up for Baby B by his parents. Based on the trust document, the funds in the trust should be placed in long term, investment grade bonds. Mr. T, the trust manager, was offered by a colleague, to invest the money in a new equity mutual fund. Though Mr. T sees the potential in the new fund, he knows that he can't put any money from the trust fund into that.

Example 2: Mr. B, a savvy investor, believes that the stock prices of Company ABC and XYZ will fall within the next few months. He believes that the best way to make money from the decline in prices is to short sell both stocks. Unfortunately for Mr. B, short selling is illegal in the local stock exchange.

Example 3: Dr. M is the medical director of a large multinational pharmaceutical company, MNO. Their latest anti-hypertensive product, Hypoten, which they tout as a "revolutionary" drug, may fail to secure FDA approval. Once this news gets out, Dr. M knows that the stock price of MNO is going to decline drastically. If Dr. M acts on this information, he violates insider trading laws.

Example 4: Mr. R and his friends are planning to put up a restaurant. They expect the business to be highly profitable. They expect to use half of the profits to grow the business and the other half to distribute amongst themselves. They are undecided as to whether to put up a partnership or a corporation. Their lawyer advised them to put up a corporation because of the better legal protection. In case of a lawsuit (e.g. from creditors or clients), their liability is limited to the assets of the corporation. Their personal properties will be spared.

Tax Considerations

Investors will naturally choose investments that are advantageous tax-wise. This strategy falls under **tax avoidance,** which is legal, and refers to strategies in utilizing the tax regime's laws to lessen tax burden. This is different from **tax evasion,** which is illegal, and refers to strategies to not pay the correct taxes.

Example 1: Mr. S decides to place his money in interest bearing deposit accounts. If he holds his money in those accounts for five years, he will be exempted by law from paying the 20% withholding tax on interest earned. Since he is investing with a long term objective, he opts to place his money in the five year accounts.

Example 2: Mr. R and his friends are planning to put up a restaurant. They expect the business to be highly profitable. They expect to use half of the profits to grow the business and the other half to distribute amongst themselves. They are undecided as to whether to put up a partnership or a corporation. Their financial adviser told them that a partnership is tax-advantageous. The profits in a partnership are taxed only once (as income to the individual partners) while the profits in a corporation are taxed twice (first as income of the corporation, and second as income to the individual partners upon distribution as dividends). Mr. R and his friends chose to put up a partnership.

Trading in the stock exchange offers investors tax advantages.

Example 3: Mr. S plans to buy and sell stocks. Publicly traded stocks which meet the minimum float requirement is subject to a stock transaction tax of 0.5% of the gross selling price. These stocks are also exempt from documentary stamp taxes (DST). All other kinds of stocks are subject to net capital gains tax between 5-10% and DST of PHP 0.75 for every PHP 200. Because of the tax advantages, Mr. S invests in the stock market.

Estate planning is probably one of the more popular areas where tax considerations factor heavily on decision making.

Example 4: Mr. O wants to transfer ownership of his house to his son. The property has an appraised value (for tax purposes) of PHP 10 million. The estate tax will amount to 1.215 million. However, if he decides to donate the property to his son, the donor's tax will amount to 1.04 million. If he decides to "sell" the property to his son for a token amount, the total tax due based on the appraised value is 750 thousand. Mr. O chose the last option.

Example 5: Mr. Y wants to bequeath his fortune to his daughter. He decides to divert some of his funds to buy a life insurance policy. In case of his death, the payout from the insurance claim is tax-exempt.

Unique Circumstances

These refers to all the remaining factors that may influence an investor's decision.

Example 1: Mr. G considers himself as an environmentalist. His stockbroker recommends mining and oil stocks. He refuses to buy these stocks because he believes that mining and oil companies contribute greatly to the degradation of the environment.

Example 2: Mrs. S sold her shares of property development company XYZ despite optimistic price projections. XYZ was in the news lately for displacing indigenous tribes in order to put up a resort complex.

STEP 5. Develop an investment plan.

Based on the return and risk objectives, and the five constraints; an investor and his financial adviser can develop an investment plan. The investment strategies may be documented via an Investment Policy Statement (IPS)

Documentation of the strategies via the IPS helps both the investor and his advisers/agents stick to the overall investment plan.

Example: Dr. D is a 35 year old physician. He just started his practice five years ago and considers his practice and income as stable. He pegs his income growth with that of inflation. He plans to retire by age 65. He is unmarried and does not plan to do so.

He only supports himself . His goal is to finance his retirement, maintaining the lifestyle that he currently has. He believes he will live until age 85. Since he expects to have no heirs upon his death, he doesn't care about leaving something behind. If he still has some money left over after his death, it will probably be donated to charities or bequeathed to close relatives.

He earns about 3,000,000 annually (after taxes). His expenses amount to about 2,000,000 with 500,000 (both adjusted for taxes) of that work related. He expects his expenses to grow with inflation through the years.

He currently rents an apartment. He plans to buy his own house in 10 years with a budget of 12 million (at present value). He has savings of 4 million (with 1% annual interest) and has no debt. His share of the family inheritance may be around 3 million (at present value).

Since he only earns when he works, he's worried about things that may prevent him from working.

When asked about his risk tolerance, he claims he has high risk tolerance; though he specifies that he doesn't want to lose money at any point. He feels that he may not earn that back. His marginal income tax rate is 32%. He prefers to invest in health related stocks because that is his field. Inflation is expected at 3% for the long term

Return Objective

- Have enough money for retirement (for 20 years covering age 65-85) to maintain current lifestyle. He currently spends 1.5 million on himself. Work related expenses should be excluded since he won't be spending these upon retirement. Expenses at retirement should be adjusted for inflation
- Buy a house in 10 years worth 12 million (at present value)
- Bequest is not a priority
- Inflation is at 3% annually

Risk Objective

Ability: He has high ability to tolerate risk for the following reasons:

- He earns more than he spends and the disparity is expected to grow with inflation.
- His income is stable.
- He has savings and no debt.
- He has potential inheritance of 3 million.
- He is 30 years away from retiring.

Willingness: He is sending mixed signals. He states that he has high risk tolerance but says he doesn't want to lose money. Since his reason for not wanting to lose money is the fear of not regaining it back (which is unlikely for his profile), the adviser can easily counsel him about it.

Overall: High risk tolerance

Constraints

Time Horizon

His investment horizon is multi-staged. The first stage is from now until he purchases his house, which is 10 years. The second stage is from that point until his retirement, which is 20 years. The third stage is from retirement onwards which is another 20 years.

Liquidity Constraints

He is planning to buy a house in the next 10 years worth 12 million. He will have to put off investing in his retirement fund until after this purchase. This is why the start of the period for which he invests for retirement will be 10 years from now.

Legal Constraints

There are none stated

Tax Consideration

Philippine tax laws apply.

Unique Circumstances

Personal injuries or disabilities may prevent him from earning. Malpractice suits may potentially eat up his personal wealth.

His income may not be as stable as he thinks. Since he is just starting his practice, his income may still grow significantly. In later years, his income may actually decline due to the influx of more competition. Potential issues regarding his reputation may also affect his income.

Though he prefers to invest in health related stocks, this action is not recommended. To reduce overall asset risk, he should invest in sectors different from his line of work.

Advice: Dr. D should take out a loan to buy the house now, instead of saving up for it.

It is probably best to buy the house at present to lock the price at current values. House prices may rise significantly in ten years. He can use his 4 million savings as downpayment and take out a loan on the balance.

Eight million amortized at 8% annual interest will result in annual payments of 1.192 million for 10 years (computation of amortization payments is not covered in this book though apps and software exist for this purpose; for simplicity, I based the computation on annual payments, instead of monthly).

Given that Dr. D only has current excess income of 1 million, it may appear that he cannot afford the mortgage. However, the payments are already fixed for the next 10 years, so they will NOT rise with inflation. Dr. D's excess income is expected to rise with inflation and will reach 1.19 million at age 41. Since Dr. D is currently renting, his expenses will be reduced when he acquires his own house. Therefore, Dr. D will be able to afford the mortgage. If Dr. D gets a better loan term, the payments will be lower.

Dr. D should get a loan with a prepayment option. If he earns more, he can prepay the principal balance in full and save on further interest payments.

Dr. D will start investing for his retirement after the house is fully paid. The return objective should be set higher while he is working and be lowered when he retires. I can set a return objective at 7% (net of taxes) pre-retirement, and 3% (net of taxes) during retirement. The fund growth should at least match inflation during retirement. If he decides to sell his house during retirement and if he receives his inheritance, the return objectives can be set lower in both stages.

Asset Allocation Strategy for Dr. D

First Stage - Since Dr. D has amortization payments, he is advised to hold his money in cash, treasury bills, commercial paper or money market funds.

Second Stage - Since Dr. D is investing for retirement, and the set objective is 7%, Dr. D can allocate his funds into different asset classes which collectively may yield 7% or more after taxes. Cash and bonds may not be enough to satisfy this return objective. Dr. D will have to invest in high risk assets A combination of cash, bonds, stocks and alternative investments may yield the return objective.

Third Stage - The return objective is set lower at 3% Some of the funds can then be shifted into low risk assets. A higher proportion of bonds in the portfolio may yield this rate.

The house should be included in the overall portfolio. However, if Dr. D decides to live in the house until his death and bequeath it to someone, the house can be excluded from the portfolio. When Dr. D receives his inheritance, this should be invested in the portfolio as well.

Rule of Thumb Asset Allocation Strategies

60-40 Stocks: Bonds

This is a popular strategy. Unfortunately, this is a one-size-fits-all strategy and may not be appropriate for everyone's profile. In the given example, this rule in inappropriate for Dr. D in the first stage. This strategy also excludes alternative investments.

100-Minus-Age Stock Allocation

This strategy suggests that you invest, as percentage of your portfolio, the difference between 100 and your age, to equities. A 45 year old will have to invest 55 % of his portfolio to stocks. A 35 year old will have to invest 65% of his assets to stocks. A retiree at age 65 will have to invest just 35% of his assets to stocks.

Though this strategy is dynamic and may actually end up being appropriate, age is just one of many factors in setting an asset allocation strategy. Again, this strategy excludes alternative investments.

Advice: Since Dr. D has no dependents nor heirs, he doesn't need life insurance. He may need to take out disability, accident, health, property and malpractice insurance.

STEP 6. Invest, monitor investments, and make adjustments accordingly.

To start investing, an investor can contact an investment firm, bank, or any institution which can provide him access to the asset classes in his strategy.

If investments fulfill both return and risk objectives, minimal adjustments need to be done. However, expected returns on different asset classes can easily change, so the investor needs to adjust his portfolio based on these new expectations. As the specific assets earn at different rates, the proportion of the portfolio may also change. If the changes are significant, the investor will have to rebalance the portfolio.

An investor should set appropriate benchmarks for his strategy. If the portfolio is consistently underperforming its benchmarks, the investor may need to change his specific investments per asset class. If necessary, he may have to replace his fund manager.

The investor should update his investment plan when his circumstances change. In the given example, if Dr. D gets married and has children, his strategy will have to be significantly revised.

4

SOME CAVEATS IN INVESTING

Investment scams often come with obvious warning signs
which victims often ignore.

*"The money's the same, whether you earn it
or scam it. "*
- Bobby Heenan

If it's too good to be true, it probably is.

A low-risk, high-return investment does not exist. Even if it did, it only did so temporarily since investors would have easily taken advantage of it thereby removing it from the market.

Example: Mr. S was recruited by Ms. R to join an investment scheme. Mr. S needs to put up PHP 100,000 to the scheme. His investment is guaranteed to earn 30% monthly. To enhance his earnings, Mr. S needs to recruit investors. Mr. S received his earnings for the first month but checks for subsequent months bounced.

The above example is a pyramid investment scheme. Sure, high returns can be made, and many people have actually earned high returns. The problem is that this is not a low risk investment. In fact, the risk that there will not be enough downline investors to sustain the scheme is very high.

Bargains do exist in the market. As I mentioned in the subject of liquidity, a seller may sell an illiquid asset for much lower than its fair value to facilitate the sale. However, the investor should exercise due diligence in evaluating potential bargains. Really good bargains are rare and may require considerable effort and costs to find.

Information is money.

Reliable investment information translates to earnings. When an investor has access to reliable information ahead of others, that investor can trade ahead of others and make more money than subsequent investors. However, there is too much information out there; separating the good from the bad is a task in itself. Data may also be conflicting. Because of the internet, some financial information are readily available. Unfortunately for smaller investors, more comprehensive financial information have significant costs. These information also have to be interpreted by experts, and this adds to the costs. Large investors, which can afford to pay for these information and the analysts who will interpret them, will obviously have market advantage over smaller investors.

This is the reason why technical analysis is popular among smaller investors. Technical analysis requires less information than full-blown fundamental analysis.

An investor can always join an investment pool (such as a mutual fund) to enjoy the benefits of the information advantage mutual fund managers have over smaller investors.

An investor should not overpay for information. If the capital is relatively small and the expected gains are not significant, high information costs may result in negative returns.

Always do your computations, or have someone capable do them for you.

Some high earning investments may come with significant transaction costs, commissions, taxes, etc. These investments may also come with high opportunity costs.

An investor who thinks he's earning a lot, may not actually do so when the final computations come in. An investor should have someone perform the necessary computations when evaluating investment alternatives.

Example: Mr. M was invited to invest in asset ABC, which was expected to earn 10% annually. He was also invited to invest in asset XYZ, which was expected to earn only 7% annually. Mr. M invested his money in asset ABC right away. Mr. M then realized that his net gains with ABC was only 6% after subtracting transaction fees, management fees and taxes. Asset XYZ, a tax-advantaged investment, would have netted Mr. M 5%. Since ABC was a high risk asset, Mr. M realized that the extra 1% return was not worth the investment.

Computations should also consider cash flows. Some investments may have significant paper gains but very little actual cash inflow.

Gains on investments denominated in various currencies may vary depending on the base currency or the calculation technique used.

Do not separate your money into different mental accounts.

No money is more valuable or more special than others. Investors should not mentally separate their money into different accounts and treat them differently. Investors should think that all their money and assets form one big pile. The total portfolio should be considered when making investment decisions.

Example 1: Ms. B earns PHP 50,000 monthly and this amount is just enough to cover her expenses. She has credit card debt of PHP 50,000. At the end of the year, Ms. B is expected to receive a PHP 50,000 bonus. Instead of paying her debt, she plans to spend the bonus on a designer handbag. She treats the bonus as more special than her regular income. In doing so, Ms. B's debt grows more because of additional interest and financial charges.

Example 2: Ms. A is setting up a retirement fund. Mr. F, her financial planner, learned that she has another house that she never uses. Mr. F thinks that the property can be liquidated to provide additional funds for her portfolio. Ms. A disagrees with Mr. F. Since that is the house where her parents grew up, she feels very emotionally attached to the property. She has no plans selling the property nor converting it to an income-generating one. In the meantime, the property's maintenance and tax costs continue to eat up a significant portion of Ms. A's money.

Follow the money trail.

It is important for investors to trace where the actual gains come from. This helps the investor in earning higher returns by moving up the money chain. In cases where the money source is questionable; by following the money trail, the investor avoids being scammed.

Example 1: Ms. B was invited to invest in a "get-rich quick", high earning, low risk scheme. Ms. B just needs to invest PHP 100,000 to the fund and she will be guaranteed a 30% monthly return. Ms. B did her research before investing. She found out that the earnings from the scheme will just come from the funds placed by new investors. There was no legitimate business underlying the scheme. She is also surprised at how the recruiters can offer a 30% monthly return when most legitimate investments only earn around 10% annually. Ms. B concludes that the scheme is just another pyramid scam.

Example 2: Milk tea shops are sprouting up everywhere and Ms. B was invited to invest in Milk Tea Shop Inc. (MTSI). Ms. B did her research. She found out that these shops are profitable, but as more shops open, she expects profitability to decline. She found out about another company, Tea Supplies Inc. (TSI), which sells supplies to most milk tea shops in the metropolis. As more shops open, TSI gains more clients and earns more money. Ms. B decides to invest in TSI instead of MTSI.

Sometimes, investors can be swayed by financial advisers or by the companies themselves. By following the money trail, investors can decipher the true motives of such entities.

Example 3: Condominium Developer (CD) is marketing a new residential condominium. Agents of CD tell prospective buyers that condo units are good investments since a lot of money can be made from eventually renting out the units. Ms. B was one of those prospects. If a lot of money is to be made from residential rentals, she wonders why CD doesn't directly rent out the condos they build. Ms. B wonders why CD has to sell the condos if the buyers will end up making more money via rental income.

CD also builds malls and office buildings but the units in those buildings are never sold but are rented out directly by CD. Ms. B comes to the conclusion that renting out commercial and office units is very lucrative, while renting out residential units is not as lucrative. This is why CD sells residential units instead of renting them out. CD will earn more profits in selling than in renting out residential units. Upon realizing how shrewd CD is, Ms. B bought shares of CD, instead of buying their condo unit.

Distinguish between salesmen and investment advisers.

There are people who give out investment advice, then let the client choose from a wide variety of investment options. There are also people who give out advice that somehow requires buying products or services they are selling.

There are also people who act as both. They give out advice and tell you about the variety of investment options. However, they encourage you to purchase their products or services over those of others.

Example 1: Mr. C meets up with Ms. B. He introduces himself as an investment consultant. He advises Ms. B that condominium units are very hot investments, and that she will earn from both rental income and capital appreciation.. Mr. C then gives her a brochure of the condominium units he is selling. He also tells her about the great payment schemes. He tells her to make a downpayment on a unit right now because of an impending price increase.

Example 2: Mr. I works as an investment consultant for AAA Bank. Mr. I meets with Ms. B and informs her of the mutual fund products AAA is offering. Based on Ms. B's profile, Mr. I recommends an equity mutual fund. He discusses AAA's equity fund products.

In the first example, Mr. C is clearly acting as a sales agent. A condominium unit may not even be a suitable investment for Ms. B, but that is of no concern to Mr. C, because his goal is to sell a unit.

When Ms. B buys the unit, Mr. C earns his commission. Mr. C probably does not know any other investment asset class to recommend to Ms. B except for condos. He is not required to follow up on whether Ms. B actually earns from her investment later on.

In the second example. Mr. I is acting both as a financial adviser and a seller of investment products. Though he is selling her his company's investment products, he still recommends a product that is appropriate for Ms. B. Mr. I may or may not earn a commission for selling the investment product. When Ms. B buys into the fund, Mr. I will have to monitor her investments and report to her.

There is nothing wrong with the scenario in the second example. For small time investors, this may even be the best option. Financial advice and research can be very expensive on their own, but many firms bundle these cheaply with their investment offerings.

As an investor, be aware that anybody can label themselves investment consultants and financial advisers. Determine their expertise, background, and what they'll eventually gain from their so called advice.

High growth cannot go on indefinitely.

The economy and markets go into cycles of growth, peak, and decline. Companies may experience high growth for the first few years, but as competition intensifies and the market saturates, the growth tempers. A small startup company has a lot of room to grow. This is not the case for an already large company. Financial analysts, when valuing growing companies, factor in high initial growth rates that eventually taper to lower long term future rates.

Example: Company XYZ, a startup electronics company, had an average annual growth rate of 20% over the past five years. Mr. F, a financial analyst, expects this period of high growth to last for ten more years as XYZ gains market share. After those 10 years, Mr. F expects the growth rate to taper to 5%, just a tad higher than inflation. Mr. F computes for the fair value of XYZ based on those assumptions.

Investors must be cognizant of this phenomenon and make their decisions accordingly. Investors can potentially earn more when investing in companies that will grow or are still growing. Investors buying into companies that have grown significantly over a long period of time may already be too late in cashing in on the growth wave.

Be cautious of the person with an investment secret to share (and sell).

If a person has a map to a buried treasure, why will he share it with someone else? Isn't it more sensible for that person to dig the treasure himself and keep all of it? So, if a person has a "get-rich quick scheme", why will he share it instead of acting on it all by himself. That person may not have the financial means to act on that scheme (the scheme may potentially be legit), or the scheme may be a sham.

Example 1: Mr F is selling a franchise for his successful milk tea kiosk business. He tells the franchisee prospect, Ms. B, that in a year, she'll be able to recoup her investment. Ms. B asks Mr. F, *"If this milk tea franchise of yours will be profitable, why do you have to ask me to invest in it? Why can't you put up your own money and keep the profits for yourself."* Mr. F answers, *"Because I don't have enough funds to grow the business myself, I need money from outside investors. As the business grows, both of us will earn. You earn from the money you invested and I earn from all the the work I did in establishing the brand"*. Upon hearing this, Ms. B was convinced and becomes a franchisee.

Truth be told, many great business ideas are not acted upon because the people who thought of them don't have the resources.

Even successful businesses need outside investors to grow. The purpose of companies to list in the stock market is to have access to the investing public's funds to grow their businesses.

The bottom line is that the founders will always make the most money (relative to the money they invested) compared to the subsequent investors when the business grows. This is perfectly acceptable since it was the founders who took the highest risks. They deserve the highest returns.

What an investor should watch out for is when the person who is selling the investment idea hasn't taken any risk himself; or has no intentions in helping the buyer implement that idea.

Example 2: Mr. T is selling a franchise of his coffee kiosk "business" to a prospect Ms. B. Mr. T has no coffee kiosk of his own. His coffee kiosk brand is virtually unknown. Mr. T actually just sells franchises. In exchange for a franchise fee, he gives the franchisee a coffee kiosk complete with logos, signages, and equipment. The franchise also comes with an initial inventory of coffee supplies. After those have been exchanged, it is expected that Ms. B will run the business herself. She may buy additional supplies from Mr. T if she wishes.

In this example, it is obvious that Ms. B is taking all the risks. Mr. T has nothing to lose from the setup. Even if Ms. B's coffee kiosk fails, Mr. T will be unaffected. Mr. T will just move on to the next prospect and earn a new set of franchise fees. In this case, the investment scheme is dubious. Mr. T does not really sell businesses, he just sells business supplies and packages them as "franchises".

Example 3: Mr. L is holding a seminar on "Secrets in Winning the Lotto". The seminar consists of Mr. L discussing computations in predicting the lotto winning numbers. The seminar fee charged to each participant is PHP 500. Ms. B was invited by her friend to attend the seminar. She wonders why Mr. L needs to share his "secrets". Couldn't he just act on these secrets and win the lotto jackpot every week? If Mr. L had indeed won the lotto based on these secrets, why does he need to conduct a seminar to earn money? Mr. B smells a sham and decides not to attend.

There are big fishes out there. They are big and powerful.

There are "small" and "big" investors. The smallness or bigness actually depends on the amount of money one puts in. The high rollers in the investment industry are those who invest billions; majority of which are institutional investors, though there are some individual investors who can rival them in terms of assets invested.

These big investors can move markets. Large buy or sell orders from these big investors can significantly affect market prices. Even among agents or brokerage firms, they usually tend first to bigger clients. Sure, fair-dealing is the ethical way of doing things; but in reality, many agents will focus more on the bigger clients since they make more money from them than from smaller clients.

The bigger investors have better access to information. Some big investors may even have the resources to manipulate the markets at the expense of the small investors.

There is a gambling related saying - "the house always wins". This is because the "house" has an overwhelming financial advantage over any individual gambler and can bankrupt the gambler at any given point, thereby preventing him from gambling again to regain lost bets.

The same can be said about investors who take speculative positions with large institutions as counterparties. The investor may gain in some transactions, but may end up losing everything with a single bad transaction.

The large institution can absorb losses better and may keep on trading until it recovers previous losses. The small investor won't have that luxury. Small newbie investors who speculate on foreign exchange often experience this.

The good news is that many big investors are actually made up of small investors who are pooling their money. Mutual funds and pension funds are examples of these. Therefore, small investors can actually grow in power by grouping themselves and pooling their assets.

If you are a small investor who nags your broker constantly, don't be surprised if he drops you as a client. To him, you are not worth the extra effort and stress.

As a small investor, if the commissions earned from you are little, there is a danger that you might be deemed "useful" for something else. A broker may use you as a pawn to prop up stock prices in behalf of a much bigger client. A broker may also dump illiquid securities that nobody wants on your account (he'll hype those securities to you of course). As a small investor, find a broker or investment firm that you can trust, and always lookout for yourself.

Past performance is not indicative of future performance.

Investment fund products often come with this disclaimer but that doesn't stop overzealous agents/ brokers from emphasizing past performance to entice potential clients. The economy and market go into cycles. A growth period may be followed by periods of stagnation and decline.

Example 1: Mr. M meets up with Ms. B with regards to a mutual fund he is promoting, Equity Fund M (EFM). He boasts that EFM has an average annual gain of 18% over the past five years; 30% gain from the past year alone. Because of the fund's great recent performance, he tells her that this a good long term investment compared to other assets and mutual funds. However, Ms. B did her own research prior to the meeting. She found out that EFM has been in existence for 10 years and for the first five years, the fund's performance was either flat or negative. She tells Mr. M that she'll do more research before making her decision.

The better way to assess fund performance is not on its absolute yield, but on its yield as compared to benchmarks. Benchmarks can be set to compare how a specific investment performs compared to how the overall market performs. How a fund performs compared to a benchmark may indicate how good the fund manager is.

Example 2: Upon further research, Ms. B found out that similar funds with the same strategy as EFM only averaged 10% gains over the past five years. During the years when EFM had negative growth, the market itself suffered losses worse than that of EFM. Ms. B believes that EFM is managed well and decides to invest.

For specific securities, a series of price upswings may be a signal of worse things to come. A security that is performing well may eventually be deemed as overbought and overvalued by the market, which may lead to its selloff and devaluation in subsequent periods.

An overbought or overvalued security, being eventually sold off and devalued in the short term, is said to be experiencing **market correction**. In this phase, a security's price may dip lower than its intrinsic value; therefore, this is one of the best times to look for bargains.

Market correction that is going on for too long may indicate that the market is already entering a **bearish** phase. Some experts don't recommend buying securities during bear markets because prices may dip even lower. Widespread investor pessimism during bear markets make the prospect of a quick price recovery highly unlikely. However, it is not uncommon for investors to take advantage of opportunities in bear markets. The companies themselves often buy back their own shares during these periods.

Enjoy the fruits of your investments.

I had to put this in last since I feel that many people invest just for the sake of investing. Money is worthless if you don't spend it. Money is not the end. Investments are means to an end.

"When you have money, think of the time when you had none."
- Japanese Proverb

END

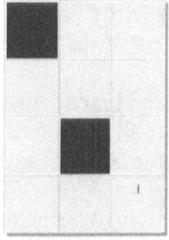

Recommended Reading

The materials in this book were sourced from a variety of books, publications, and websites that I have been reading since I started studying about investments. Here are some of the materials that I recommend to anyone interested about investing:

For general investment knowledge, news, commentary, recommendations, market quotes and other investment related information:

1. Investopedia http://www.investopedia.com/
2. Yahoo Finance http://finance.yahoo.com/
3. Investor Guide http://www.investorguide.com/
4. The Wall Street Journal http://online.wsj.com/home-page
5. Marketwatch http://www.marketwatch.com/
6. The Motley Fool http://www.fool.com/
7. The Street http://www.thestreet.com/
8. Seeking Alpha http://seekingalpha.com/

For investment planning, The CFA Level III, Volume 2 curriculum book provides a good discussion on how to formulate an investment policy statement. However, the CFA curriculum books are only available for purchase by registered CFA candidates. https://www.cfainstitute.org/

If you want to learn more about the Modern Portfolio Theory, then read the book that started it all. The book is available in newer editions and reprints

Markowitz, H.M. (1959). *Portfolio Selection: Efficient Diversification of Investment*s. New York: John Wiley & Sons.

For Philippine market information:
Philippine Stock Exchange http:// www.pse.com.ph/
Security and Exchange Commission http://www.sec.gov.ph/
Bangko Sentral ng Pilipinas http://www.bsp.gov.ph/
Bureau of Internal Revenue http://www.bir.gov.ph/

About the Author

I am a physician, and currently practice as an anesthesiologist. In 2005, I took up my MBA. It was then that I realized that I had a knack for finance. In 2008, I took up a six-month course in investment co-administered by the Philippine Stock Exchange and earned the title of Certified Securities Specialist the following year. In that course, where majority of my classmates have a degree and/or work in finance, I surprisingly topped the class. I decided to continue my journey into finance. I sought out what is probably one of the most prestigious and difficult credentials in finance, the designation of Chartered Financial Analyst or CFA. As of 2013, I have passed all three levels of the CFA exams, all in my first attempts. I have yet to receive my charter, pending completion of the required four years of investment work experience.

My Journey in the CFA Program

The CFA program consists of three levels. Each level requires months of self-study and culminates in a six hour exam. Each level is comprised of several study areas and topics that can fill out five to six books. The Level I exams are given in June and December. The exams for both Levels II and III are given only in June. I passed Level I in December 2011, Level II in June 2012 and Level III in June 2013; all of them at first attempts. One has to be committed in studying in order to pass the exams. Since I don't work in finance, I had to exert more effort. The passing rates for my specific exams were 38% (Level I, December 2011), 42% (Level II, 2012) and 49% (Level III, 2013).

Despite passing all the required exams, I am not yet eligible to receive the CFA designation. I need to complete four years of required investment work experience. I currently work as a physician, but someday, I hope to have the time to complete the requirement.

The CFA program and exams are conducted by only one entity, the CFA Institute in Virginia, USA. The same exams are given to all the candidates worldwide at practically the same days (adjusting only for time zones, so some examinees will take the exam hours ahead of the others).

Achievements in the CFA program, whether being awarded the designation or passing certain exam levels, are therefore accepted anywhere in the world. Passing the CFA exams in Manila is the same as passing them in New York or London.

The topics covered in the CFA program are as follows: Ethical and Professional Standards, Quantitative Methods, Economics, Financial Reporting and Analysis, Corporate Finance, Equity Investments, Fixed Income, Derivatives, Alternative Investments, Portfolio Management and Wealth Planning.

Although there are some physicians who have transitioned into finance, I am currently aware of only one physician who has the CFA designation. He used to be a clinician but now runs a wealth management firm in the United States. I hope to take the same path someday.

INVESTING FOR NEWBIES

What You Need to Know to Get Started

ROLAN H. CARREON M.D.
2014

Visit me at https://financemd.wordpress.com